AGELESS WISDOM
SPIRITUALITY

AGELESS WISDOM
SPIRITUALITY

Investing in Human Evolution

Andy James

To order additional copies of this book, contact:
Xlibris Corporation
1-888-795-4274
www.Xlibris.com
Orders@Xlibris.com
20079

CONTENTS

Acknowledgements 7
Foreword 9
Introduction 13
  All Quiet on the Runaway Train 13
  Making the Connections 19
  Whither America? 22
Chapter 1: The Impact of Religion and Science 29
  What's the Purpose of Life? 29
  The Triumph of Quantity over Quality 30
  Scientism: The New Religion 33
  The Costs of Free Market Morality 36
  Technology: The Future 42
  Fundamentalism, New Age Spirituality,
    and Postmodernism 49
  The Antidote: Spirituality beyond Belief 56
Chapter 2: The Hidden Effects of Technology 63
  Technology Is Not Neutral 63
  Is Reality Obvious? 65
  The Impact of Media, Culture, and Society 68
  Complexity, Stress, and the Quick Fix 78
  Alienation, Dependence, and Virtual Reality 84
  Sex, Violence, and the Sensational 89
  The Antidote: Simplicity and Inner Direction 98
Chapter 3: The Ageless Wisdom: Our Common Ground 103
  The Impact of Genesis 105
  What and Where Is Spirit? 108
  The Problem of the Separate "I" or Self 112
  The Evolution of Consciousness—Psychology,
    Psychics and Enlightenment 122

Chapter 4: Spiritual Paths and Pitfalls 134

Why Information and Reason Are Not Enough 134

Belief, Conditioning, and the Separate Self 139

Wisdom: Beyond Progress, Pain, and Pleasure 143

The Path of Devotion and the Heart 148

The Path of Action and Work.................................. 152

The Esoteric Mind-Body Path 154

In Summary... 158

Chapter 5: An Ageless Wisdom Vision.................... 162

Finding a Voice 163

The Science of Self.. 169

A Personal Journey.. 173

Morality and Law 179

Environment, Economics, Science, and Politics 183

Media.. 190

Health and Education 196

Conclusion 211

Chronology of the Ageless Wisdom 217

ACKNOWLEDGEMENTS

This book cuts across conventional attitudes and of course, established publishing niches. I am fortunate to be able to count as friends several individuals who think and live outside the predictable.

In the first place, I am grateful to V.R. Dhiravamsa not only for his excellent instruction in Vipassana and Buddhism but for introducing me, nearly thirty years ago, to the Enneagram, the works of Ken Wilber, and the use of bodywork and interactive work within the context of Vipassana meditation. I would never have thought of becoming a meditation teacher if he had not suggested it.

I would like to thank Donna Oliver, Sheila Furness, and Jeff Willis for countless stimulating and inspiring discussions during more than fifteen years of our weekly Vipassana meditation group. They echo throughout this book. I am grateful for their unwavering support as friends and pioneering students who have in their own right achieved a high level of skill in the Daoist "internal" arts of Taijiquan, Qigong, etc.

I would like to thank my partner, Nicola Lawrence, for her insightful love, enthusiastic support, good instincts, and wacky sense of humor.

To Lucinda Vardey, Patrick Crean, Emily Sell, and Lili Fournier, I am grateful for invaluable advice on the workings of the book-publishing and media worlds.

I am indebted to my mother, Beryl, for a lifetime of nurturing and good cheer and for being a perfect grandmother to my children.

I am grateful to my brothers Michael, Ray and Brian for always supporting the structure of our extended family.

I am grateful to my daughters, Shuwen, Shuwei, and Hana, for being precisely who they are—vibrant, independent, insightful, loving, and unique. I dedicate this book to them and to all future generations.

FOREWORD

Here is another highly inspiring book written with a great clarity and broad scope by Andy James who, in addition to his mastery over Tai Chi Chuan and Qi Gong, received a complete training course under my instruction and guidance some fifteen years ago. It was a period of time from 1982 to 1992 that I established and directed the **Vipassana (Insight) Meditation Center** on San Juan Island, State of Washington. During that significant time Andy was the one who was keenly interested in receiving a full training in this method of the Unique Buddhist Meditation known as Vipassana. He did it well and accomplished his studies in all the teachings related to Vipassana and its practice so that he could impart his knowledge and experience far and wide in North America, particularly in Canada, the country where he and his family live.

After reading his new book, **"Ageless Wisdom Spirituality: Investing in Human Evolution,"** I am given a new perspective regarding the synthesis of Religion and Science, the effects of technology over our modern lives in the globalized world, our common ground on genesis, spirit, and evolution of consciousness. In addition, Andy clearly and precisely points out the spiritual paths that include devotional practice and awakening of the heart, together with some pitfalls in which many, so-called spiritual people submerge themselves, and therefore replace the middle way with a "muddle path". This is pretty much like an elephant sinking in the mud.

[1]By synthesis I mean the bringing together, the reconciling, and the bridging of those two worldviews so that the harmony in co-existence, the mutual understanding with regard to cultures and religions, and the genuine respect for one another through honoring, accepting, and embracing *concepts and meanings* employed by either world. It is the act of synthesizing the concepts that can bring about some deep insights into the Eastern Mind and the Western View. This is for the reason that the old patterns of viewing and looking at things may be radically changed for creating the *peaceful and harmonious* co-existence in our contemporary world in which the modern psyche manifests on the friendly and reconciling terms. That is to say, the old psyche tends toward killing and destroying the dragon (opposite) when encountering it, while our modern psyche moves toward bringing the dragon home so that the reconciling process can begin and the two worlds will be brought together in synthesis.

Bear in mind that we *are* the world, and this concept "world," both in the East and the West represents our existence that consists of the *five aggregates* that make up our humanness and divinity. Those five aggregates are *physical body, sensation/feeling, perception and ideation, concoction and activity, and consciousness.* All the manifestations in the world come from each of us and are directed by us human beings both individually as a person and collectively as a group, a society, a culture, and a nation. We relate to one another according to our ways and means that are conditioned and molded by our cultures, religions, belief systems, and/or personal experiences. Whenever and anywhere in the world the manifestation takes place, be it social, political, economical, or religious, it represents our relationships to one another, to a certain situation, to environment, or to the world at large. We create the

---

[1] The following two paragraphs are taken from the author's (Dhiravamsa's) unpublished in English manuscript entitled: A New Vision of Buddhism. Nonetheless, it has been published in Spanish language by Ediciones La Llave, Vitoria, Spain.

world. We *are* the creators either of peace or war, harmony or conflict, friendship or enemy, friendly intercourse or violence, etc. We are *responsible* for whatever happens in the world, in which we live and manifest our individual or collective consciousness, or unconscious driving forces for that matter. When we lay blames on one another, we are in fact attempting to escape the responsibility since blaming is an easy way out, although it's not a solution, while taking responsibility costs us tremendous energy, time, and wisdom to find the real solution to our challenges. As we know, responsibility is the ability to respond (response + ability) realistically and totally. If each of us uses all our possible human resources, including the ability to respond wisely to any situations or circumstances, we are actually able to solve any problems and to make peace together. As a result, we all can live together in peace and in harmony, surpassing all the unwelcoming conflicts and insecurity in our beloved world.

Certainly, the practice of spirituality requires a great deal of **attention, awareness, and creative presence** in which operates adequately our **aware ego** (an executive function of personality and psyche) so that things in life and in the world will be carried out with an open, positive attitude. With such an attitude and the right practice one will succeed in raising consciousness and in transforming the negative/destructive, dark forces.

I do hope that the reader will find, as I do, this present work of Andy James inspiring, clarifying, and pointing to the treasures both within and outside.

May you all be well and happy!

Dhiravamsa
L'Escala, Gerona
Spain

INTRODUCTION

All Quiet on the Runaway Train

"There's too much to do and not enough time!" is by far the most common complaint I hear. In spite of this, however, people continue to undertake ever more activity, and as a result, the pace of life accelerates.

Although we have grown accustomed to this phenomenon, it is neither harmless nor insignificant, but the result of extremely powerful and complex forces, which we will examine in this book. For the moment, it should be noted that there are two important effects of chronic time pressure. In the first place, although "non-specific," it can lead to serious health problems. Stress-related diseases are now regarded as the preeminent health threat in developed countries.

The second (and largely unacknowledged) effect of time pressure is that it so enervates us we have neither the inclination nor energy to inquire into the quality and direction of our collective lives. As we understandably seek solace and escape in the "cocoon" of our private lives, the field is left wide open to those with an agenda to push through. The problem is compounded by the fact that as society rapidly becomes more complex, it is increasingly difficult for individuals to understand, much less influence, what is taking place. Even a cursory examination of public opinion polls will reveal inconsistent, volatile, and therefore malleable attitudes. Social change is largely driven by scientific and technological innovation, which in turn is largely driven by greed and vanity. The current Free Market motto seems to be: "Make your profits before your competitor does and get out before the true costs (to society) become evident." The most effective deterrent to corporate piracy seems to be legal action, but the law usually lags years behind current market realities and is thus often a case of shutting the proverbial barn door after the horse has bolted.

The result is that our lives, both individual and collective, often feel like a runaway train gathering speed. The "optimists" (seemingly in the majority) insist that the track ahead is straight and level and that it will speed us all to sci-fi Utopia. They dismiss as "negative" and "dreamers" those who question the purpose and destination of the journey or raise the possibility that there may be sharp turns or broken track ahead. Thus, even though highly qualified and dedicated experts from many walks of life are sounding urgent alarm bells, the majority of the populace in (still insulated) America is unstirred. To me this is as disturbing as the problems themselves, because without taking the first step, there can be no movement towards a solution. The more we delay, the more dangerous is our predicament and the less time there is to attempt a remedy.

Hereunder are three major, interconnected areas of concern, which need to be urgently addressed, regardless of whether we see ourselves as optimistic or pessimistic, hardheaded or idealistic, left or right wing. Terrorism is certainly a grave concern but does not deserve our current obsession since it is neither separate from nor more important than these issues and should not be used as a red flag to divert us to ill-considered actions.

1.   *The Health of the Planet.*

Many people simply refuse to believe that anything as big and old as the earth can really suffer any serious damage. Everything is relative, however, including space and time. Pollution and demands on the earth's resources have been increasing exponentially. In 1825, the world's population for the first time ever reached the 1-billion mark. In just one hundred years (1925), it had doubled to 2 billion, and it took a mere fifty more years (1975) to double again to 4 billion. By 1990, world population had reached 5.3 billion. The World Bank estimates the global population will stabilize at 10-11 billion in about fifty years, but other sources suggest 14-15 billion. Most people will flock to congested megacities of 15 million and more, looking for work and survival.

Thanks to the successful marketing of Western consumerism, each person now expects not only water, food, and shelter but also power, transportation, consumer goods, entertainment, etc. All of this requires enormous amounts of land and resources and generates corresponding amounts of garbage, pollution, and long-lasting toxicity, which is extremely difficult for the planet to assimilate. The waste from atomic energy, touted as "cheap" and "clean," remains radioactive for 100,000 years!

Those expecting scientific "miracles" conveniently forget that many of our current problems have resulted from innovations that were in their own times touted as miracles—power and chemical plants, atomic energy and weapons, motor vehicles, roads, large-scale deforestation, farming and fishing, fertilizers, pesticides, preservatives, additives, hormones, etc. Even antibiotics are losing their effectiveness as new "super" strains of microorganisms mutate.

Danger signs of staggering proportions abound but are routinely ignored. Species of flora and fauna are dying off at a rate (over 30,000 per year) not seen since the extinction of the dinosaurs 65 million years ago. Biologists are calling this phenomenon the "sixth extinction". A large asteroid wiped out the dinosaurs and ice ages were responsible for the other four previous extinctions. At the same time, global warming, with its alarming and widespread implications, is increasing at a rate not experienced within the last 100 million years. An iceberg the size of Wisconsin, which broke off the Antarctic ice shelf, merited mere single column, inside page coverage in most newspapers.

In 2002, The U.N. Environment Program (UNEP) released a 450-page report based on the work of over 1,000 scientists. It concluded that the planet was in imminent danger, and the worst-case scenario would be for us to continue our present "market first" approach. The executive director of UNEP, Klaus Toepfer, warned, "It would be a disaster to sit back and ignore the picture that is painted."

2. The Poverty Gap

Despite much talk about globalization bringing unprecedented worldwide prosperity, the gap between the rich and the poor (both within individual countries and between countries) has been increasing since the mid-1960s. There is actually a net flow of money from the poorer countries to the richer countries, and this has increased within the last two decades. About half the world's population (about 3 billion) still relies on agriculture for their main source of income and of these, 1 billion are subsistence farmers. Over 1 billion people lack access to clean drinking water. Famines in Africa and Asia have killed millions at a time.

Technological innovation, especially advances in information and communication, has accelerated the widening of the poverty gap and has concentrated a vast amount of power into a handful of corporations and individuals, mostly in the West. Since this power includes control over much of the mass media, corporations can unduly influence governments and political parties not only directly with "contributions," "sponsorships," and promises of job creation, but also by powerfully shaping the opinions of the voting public. Large corporations, some with bigger budgets than most countries, can also exert enormous leverage by threatening to move their operations or assets to other less-regulated countries. In America, CEOs and directors of large corporations often move in and out of the highest government posts with such regularity it has become an informal, albeit exclusive, club, which dangerously blurs the boundaries of duty, responsibility and honor.

The growing poverty gap not only contradicts the humanitarian ideals to which most of the West pays lip service, it fuels discontent, mistrust, hopelessness, and rage. TV has made this disparity even more galling since even the poorest person can see and hear how the wealthy and privileged live and think. For many suffering from woefully inadequate water supplies, food, housing, medicine, etc., such lifestyles are seen as wasteful, frivolous, decadent, and unjust. This is extremely fertile ground for extremist agitators of any ilk— racist, religious or political. The most dangerous and desperate are those who have nothing to lose, and as the slums, ghettos, and refugee camps multiply, so do the ranks of the reckless. When violence does arise out of such situations, it is simplistic to simply brand it as "evil" with no logical connection to social, political, and cultural realities.

Ironically, the more powerful weapons and systems the advanced countries develop to protect themselves from threat, the more potential for destruction and massacre they eventually put into the hands of terrorists. In the current hysteria over terrorism and "weapons of mass destruction" (WMDs), we strangely ignore the fact that most of these weapons were developed by the U.S.A. in the first place and much of the technology to make them was legally exported in order to make money for American corporations. No Western leader has fully explained what is undeniable—that terrorism cannot be stopped but only limited to a certain degree. Thanks to computers and other advanced technologies, small groups or even a single (perhaps demented) individual can now cause death and destruction on a large scale. That being the case, it is difficult to see the logic of trying to defeat (mostly Islamic) terrorism by invading two Islamic countries—Afghanistan and Iraq—with the inevitable consequence of killing thousands of innocent civilians and destroying vital infrastructure. Will this not recruit hundreds or perhaps thousands more terrorists who already think (correctly or not) that the U.S.A. rides rough shod over the rights of other countries, especially Islamic ones?

Poverty, inequality, conflict, and terrorism are the result of human behavior. Expecting technology to magically solve such problems without changing our attitudes and behavior is sheer folly.

3. The Implementation of Science and Technology

The runaway momentum of science and technology is the third major threat in our lives and, as we have seen above, also plays an important part in the other two. This has been the predominant force in the world over the last 400 years and remains so today. It not only shapes our physical world and the way we live but also our attitudes and the way we think. It is not a coincidence that human beings appear to have become more materialistic and mechanistic, because that is how we are training ourselves.

Scientific and technological innovations are largely uncontrolled and unexamined, especially as regards their generalized impact on society and the environment. The reasons for this will be examined in detail later in this book, but here we will briefly mention but a few. We have come to look to science for salvation (especially the "quick fix") the way we once did in regard to religion; we tend to ignore side effects that are complex, hard to measure, or costly for those trying to introduce and profit from the new technology; proof of ill effects often comes to light long after implementation and is often covered up while there are still profits to be made; we have become addicted to technology; many legislators and regulators simply do not understand the implications of new technology or are generally sympathetic to innovators and entrepreneurs.

The consequences of error, terror, and abuse grow apace with the power of technology, which in the twenty-first century will grow exponentially. In addition, genetics, robotics, and nanotechnology have the potential to significantly alter the evolution of many of this planet's species, including human beings, within a matter of decades. These innovations will be difficult to control in the present Free Market climate since they all have ostensibly "life enhancing," commercial applications rather than outright military ones. The race to market scientific or technological "breakthroughs" and reap the ensuing fortunes militate against adequate testing and control, especially since many of these are being pushed through by mighty, influential transnational corporations. Military applications of technology have always been hard to control because of the "arms race" mentality, and the present century will be no different except for the almost inconceivable potential of the new weapons.

Making the Connections

All of the above problems, not to mention the many brutal and devastating military conflicts taking place around the globe, are the result of human attitudes and decision making, not random accidents or sheer bad luck. We already have the necessary resources, information, and technology to remedy these problems. We just need the collective will to do so. It is that simple . . . and that difficult.

Although we certainly need "external" social and technical systems to organize our lives—treaties, laws, regulations, taxes, funding, education, etc.—we as individuals and as societies must also (perhaps firstly) cultivate the will to care and to share. This is an age-old and widespread dilemma made far more difficult by the fact that modern society is predominantly driven by "me first" competition and short-term gain. The average person works by this credo all day and is bombarded by it through the popular media at night in the form of "entertainment." Although a part of us understands what is right, there is a sort of disconnection and alienation occurring. A 2001 *Time Magazine* poll on global warming found that almost 80 percent of Americans (the richest and most extravagant energy consumers on the planet) did, indeed, regard global warming as a serious problem, yet less than half were willing to make minor financial sacrifices to help solve the problem.

With the rise of modern science over the last 400 years, we have increasingly looked to science and technology for external solutions to our problems and correspondingly have neglected our inner (spiritual) life and responsibilities. This is a dangerous reversal of priorities since in actual fact all external activities arise out of internal intention. Although we hate to admit it, most of us live according to largely unexamined attitudes, beliefs, habits, and desires. Instead of inquiring into the appropriateness of our behavioral patterns, we tend to hold them as sacred and look to technology to support them. We can observe this dynamic in all of the problem areas mentioned above—the poverty gap, the environmental crisis, the clash of ideologies, religions, races, cultures and nations, and of course our addiction to technology.

While the tools and weapons we wield have grown enormously in their potential, we have remained relatively static in our own development as human beings, and this has created a dangerous imbalance. Readers do not have to cast their minds back too many years to find numerous examples of leaders of powerful countries, who have acted impulsively, childishly, or insanely (often with the support of their people at that time), causing needless damage and suffering of unprecedented proportions.

Another (largely unacknowledged) reason that science and technology are slipping out of our control is that they make life increasingly complex and fragmented. There are so many issues and responsibilities to track, coordinate, and prioritize we often become overwhelmed, either turning off our attention and caring or making decisions just for the sake of making a decision, which in fact is gambling. This is ironic since a common presumption about technology is that it makes life easier and saves time. Studies have shown that this presumption is often misguided. Manufacturers not only make extravagant claims but deliberately build obsolesce and multiple add-ons to tie customers to their products. They of course minimize possible negative side effects or ignore them altogether. This may make good conventional "business sense" but is wasteful and, to many customers, unduly annoying, frustrating, time-consuming, and of course expensive.

Although experts from various fields as well as many ordinary people realize that a major shift in human thinking and behavior is urgently required, there are few suggestions as to how this might realistically occur. The politically correct intelligentsia are afraid to make any qualitative judgments lest they be accused of discrimination, and thus calls for moral and spiritual renewal are coming mostly from the religious fundamentalists, brandishing their respective sacred books as the literal, undeniable "Word of God."

This latter approach is plagued by two basic problems, which have manifested throughout history. Firstly, they lead to polarization, extremism, and often war, which is extremely unwise given the powerful weaponry now available. Fundamentalism and indeed popular religion, as we know it, have not and cannot bring humanity together in peace and harmony because their goal is the salvation of only the believers or chosen. Secondly, popular religion cannot lead to self-transformation or a radical shift in consciousness because it does not ask its adherents for it—only to obey the "word of god" as interpreted by members of the established, religious hierarchy. In this sense, popular religious belief is an imposed external system, not very different from secular laws.

Astonishingly, there has existed for thousands of years a type of spirituality, known variously as Perennial, Ageless, or Primordial Wisdom Spirituality, that would seem to be the perfect solution to the problems outlined above. It advocates self-transformation (of consciousness) based on the realization that all life is in fact interconnected and parts of a whole. As we become more "enlightened," we will see these connections more clearly and directly and will therefore respond to life's challenges with far greater spontaneity and aptness, without having to wait for cumbersome studies, theories, and laws that are years or decades too late. If each person takes more responsibility for himself/herself and makes wiser and more compassionate choices, the need for laws, police, surveillance, armies, hospitals, etc., will diminish dramatically.

Friction and conflict will lessen as we begin to see life in a more fluid, interconnected, and multi-layered manner. The rigid dividing lines between the various pairs of "opposites" will begin to blur—human and divine, internal and external, good and evil, black and white, human and animal, etc. It will be impossible to ignore the suffering of other human beings, of animals, and of the planet because we will see as a matter of clear fact (rather than idealism) that the destiny of all is intertwined.

I have described the existence of the Ageless Wisdom as "astonishing" not only because of its profundity but also because it has existed in all major cultures over the ages and yet has left

such little conscious imprint on the general populace. It has been
suggested that the general level of consciousness in the past was
not high enough to appreciate it, but perhaps we are now ready to
explore it and thus begin a major transformation of our
consciousness. This notion as well as other aspects of the Ageless
Wisdom will be discussed later. The Ageless Wisdom would include
(but not be limited to) Hinduism, Buddhism, Daoism, and the
mystic sects of the Western religions, e.g., the Christian Gnostics,
the Jewish Kabbalists, and the Islamic Sufis. Huston Smith, one of
the world's foremost authorities on religion, writes in his book,
Forgotten Truth: The Common Vision of the World's Religions:

> Since reality exceeds what science registers, we must look for
> other antennae to catch the wavebands it misses. What other
> antennae are there? None more reliable than the convergent
> sensibilities of, in Lovejoy's characterization, "the greater
> number of the subtler speculative minds and of the great
> religious teachers" that civilizations have produced . . . . It is
> the vision philosophers have dreamed, mystics have seen
> and prophets have transmitted.

Whither America?

The validity of Ageless or Perennial Wisdom spirituality does
not depend on the particulars of a certain time, place, people, or
culture—that is why it is called the Ageless Wisdom. This does
not mean, however, that in our everyday lives we are unaffected by
what happens around us or what we do has no consequence, since
most of us measure our lives in relatively short periods of years or
even months.

When I first started writing this book over three years ago, I
wrote it for all people but in particular for Americans since, with
the collapse of the Soviet Union, the U.S.A. was left as the sole
superpower and hence *de facto* world leader. The cold war was over,
and American popular culture and Free Market economics were
sweeping over the planet. If we were to tackle our collective global

problems, it seemed an ideal time for America to magnanimously lead the way, secure in its position of unchallenged military and financial strength.

American attitudes and policies, however, have shifted dramatically since the horrific terrorist attacks on September 11, 2001 that destroyed the World Trade Center towers in New York and part of the Pentagon. Within less than two years, President George W. Bush has subsequently led the U.S.A. into two "regime changing" wars in Afghanistan and Iraq, has threatened Syria, North Korea, and Iran with similar action, and has unabashedly espoused an "America first" foreign policy. The world community overwhelmingly supported the U.S. action in Afghanistan but was far more reluctant about Iraq. In the build up to the invasion of Iraq, the Bush administration brushed aside the United Nations' request for more time for existing weapons inspections and has bullied and threatened nations not willing to participate in the war, including longtime allies like France, Germany, and even Canada.

Bush's simplistic assertion that "You're either with us or against us" has struck a strong emotional and chauvinistic cord within America but has eroded the worldwide admiration, gratitude, and trust the U.S.A. had painstakingly and deservedly built up over most of the last century. The divide between American and non-American attitudes has widened, in part due to an uncritical American media. Even though Britain was America's only active military ally in the invasion of Iraq, the director general of Britain's BBC, Greg Dyke, was moved to describe the unquestioning American television and radio war coverage of the Iraq war as "shocking" and "gung-ho." He concluded that America has "no news operation strong enough or brave enough to stand up against the White House and Pentagon" and that after September 11, American networks have "wrapped themselves in the American flag and swapped impartiality for patriotism."

The most fundamental, important, and urgent decision facing Americans is whether to approach the new century trying to impose its will (*Pax Americana*) on the world or leading an initiative to cultivate an unprecedented level of global trust, harmony, sharing, and cooperation.

Although some Americans are offended by the suggestion that their country is acting like an old-fashioned empire, their own leaders have stated their intentions quite clearly. Perhaps the clearest and most comprehensive statement of intentions is contained in a lengthy 2000 report called "Rebuilding America's Defenses," which was put out by a "non-profit, educational organization" called "Project for the New American Century" (PNAC). PNAC was formed in 1997 to "promote American global leadership," and its Statement of Principles was signed by several people who would subsequently help shape and execute the policies of the George W. Bush administration—Governor of Florida Jeb Bush, who was part of the controversy surrounding the pivotal recount of presidential election votes in Florida, which his brother narrowly won, Vice-president Dick Cheney, Defense Secretary Donald Rumsfeld, and Deputy Secretary of Defense Paul Wolfowitz.

The introduction of the 2000 PNAC report states, "At present the United States faces no global rival. America's grand strategy should aim to preserve and extend this advantageous position as far into the future as possible." Among its recommendations was to develop the ability to "fight and decisively win multiple, simultaneous major theatre wars," "maintain nuclear strategic superiority," and "control the new international commons of Space and Cyberspace . . ." "In addition, there may be a need to develop a new family of nuclear weapons designed to address new sets of military requirements, such as would be required in targeting the very deep under-ground hardened bunkers being built by many of our potential adversaries . . . ." Global "constabulary" missions "demand American political leadership rather than that of the United Nations . . . Nor can the United States assume a UN-like stance of neutrality; the preponderance of American power is so great and its global interests so wide that it cannot pretend to be indifferent to the political outcome." The report prophetically warns that the process of transforming the military "is likely to be a long one, absent some catastrophic and catalyzing event—like a new

Pearl Harbor." It observes, "The Clinton Administration's adherence to the 1972 ABM Treaty has frustrated development of useful ballistic missile defenses."

The foreign policy of the Bush administration, both before and after September 11, has been remarkably in line with the above PNAC recommendations. During his election campaign, Bush bluntly asserted that America's interest should always come first and Condoleezza Rice, his eventual National Security Adviser, explained that the new administration's foreign policy would "proceed from the firm ground of national interest and not from the interest of an *illusory international community.*" America unilaterally withdrew from the Kyoto Protocol on global warming (signed by almost all the countries in the world) soon after Bush's election and subsequently from both the 1972 Anti-ballistic Missile Treaty and the World Court.

Since September 11 (the "new Pearl Harbor"), the Bush administration has been able to speedily boost funding and undertake military objectives in line with PNAC recommendations. In the section of the 2000 PNAC report entitled, "Repositioning Today's Forces," it is stated:

> The United States has for decades sought to play a more permanent role in Gulf regional security. While the unresolved conflict in Iraq provides the immediate justification, the need for a substantial American force presence in the Gulf transcends the issue of the regime of Saddam Hussein . . . Over the long term, Iran may well prove as large a threat to the U.S. interests in the Gulf as Iraq has. And even should U.S.-Iran relations improve, retaining forward-based forces in the region would still be an essential element in U.S. security strategy given the longstanding American interests in the region.

The issue of Iraq was first raised, seemingly out of nowhere, before congressional elections, just as Bush's approval ratings started to sag and was pushed through as American opinion polls eventually began to respond to rhetoric. During the Iraq war, which was ostensibly fought to get rid of "weapons of mass destruction" (as yet not found), military and administration spokespersons brazenly spoke of the possible use of "bunker busting" tactical nuclear weapons—probably to test public reaction and to gradually introduce the concept to the public. Also in line with PNAC recommendations, Americans insisted that they, not the United Nations, should control the oil revenues of the defeated Iraqis, determine who gets rebuilding contracts, and who governs in place of the deposed Saddam Hussein. The corporation, which reaped many of the most lucrative Iraqi contracts was Haliburton, the company Dick Cheney left as CEO to take up his post as vice-president and to which presumable he can return. In December, 2003, Wolfowitz rewarded those countries that supported the U.S.A. (even if only verbally) by allowing them to bid on nearly $19 billion reconstruction contracts. Those who opposed the invasion, including Canada, France, Germany and Russia, were barred ostensibly for "protection of essential security interests of the United States". This was done even as the Bush administration continued to asked those same countries for financial and military help in Iraq and even as those same countries were contributing aid and troops to the other American-led war in Afghanistan.

"What other possible response could there be to September 11? Was it not important to show strength?" it has been asked. I think it would have shown not only strength, but also maturity, wisdom, and global leadership if President Bush's response, instead of being one of cowboy swagger and revenge, was more along the lines of, "Yes, terrorists managed to hit us hard and it was a terrible tragedy, but given the size and power of our country, it is not enough to make us panic and lash out blindly. This event demonstrates the very real threat that terrorism represents to everyone on the planet and the misguided hatred in the hearts of the perpetrators, who do a disservice to their religion by murdering innocents in God's name. I am grateful for the support that countries and individuals all over the world have offered and would like to call on that support not only to cooperatively root out terrorism, by military action if necessary, but to tackle all our common global problems including repairing the environment and establishing a global safety net for those individuals and countries that have temporarily fallen on hard times. Out of the dark can come light. In this time of great shock and pain, people have spontaneously examined what is truly valuable in their lives and have started discussing the meaning of their own religion. I call on all people to continue their investigation into the true meaning of religion so that it will never be used to justify murder or if it is, all true spiritual people will rise up in condemnation. I look forward to a time when a more profound understanding of spirituality means that religion no longer divides us but shows us the way to oneness." I think a unique opportunity to build real bridges between religions and cultures was lost because revenge and power politics took priority, as it has so often in the past.

Professor Ervin Laszlo, a world expert on systems and evolution theory and a founding member of the Budapest Club, believes we only have until the end of this decade (until 2010) to determine whether we suffer Breakdown or Breakthrough. In his book, *Macroshift*, published in 2001 before September 11, he describes how Breakdown might occur:

> Rigidity and lack of foresight will lead to stresses that the established institutions can no longer contain. Conflict erupts and violence and anarchy follow in its wake.

Alternatively, we may experience a Breakthrough:

> A new way of thinking with more adapted values and more evolved consciousness will catalyze creativity in society. People and institutions learn to navigate the macro shift, mastering the stresses that arose in the wake of the previous generation's unreflective fascination with technology, wealth and power. A new era dawns: the era of a sustainable post-Logos civilization.

CHAPTER 1

THE IMPACT OF RELIGION AND SCIENCE

What's the Purpose of Life?

Asking the purpose of life is normally associated with dusty academics, bearded gurus, or comedians making fun of academics and gurus. For most people, it is "obvious" what we must do— school, education, jobs, money, cars, houses, family, holidays, "tech" toys, etc. In a competitive, fast-paced environment, we feel we must work ever faster and longer to get ahead of our competitors. "Doing" and "action" are admired, even in our leisure time. Undue thinking is frowned upon because it may cause doubt or the social discomfort of being "different," a "loner," etc. In order to progress up the company ladder, you have to play by its rules, not question them.

In fact, how we individually and collectively conduct or lives is the result of a rather haphazard interaction of behavioral patterns and beliefs, of which we are mostly unaware or unable to change. These include personality patterns, the conscious or subconscious lessons we have learned from our personal experiences (including very early childhood), education, religion, nationality, etc. In addition, individual and collective patterns continually interact and influence each other. Thus when some person or corporation professes only to be reflecting popular opinion or demand, that is only half the truth. What is put before a mass audience, whether representative of them or not, in turn impacts that audience.

Even though our specific packages of habits and beliefs are of uncertain and largely unexamined origin, we nevertheless tend to defend them fiercely. "That is me. I am proud of my individuality, and no one is going to tell me what to do!" Members of specific races, social groups, religions, and countries are similarly defensive, often using the words "sacred" and "holy" to elevate the status of their particular beliefs. Conflict and war result when belief systems collide. Much of this is unnecessary and eminently avoidable, especially since these patterns of behavior and belief are subtly changing all the time anyway.

It is astonishing that at a time when we are radically altering the face of the planet, we care so little about exploring our own internal universe. For the sake of what is "good" for human beings (especially in the prosperous West), we have devastated the planet, brought ourselves to the brink of nuclear destruction, and are now beginning to tamper with the genetic makeup of many species including humans.

Some of the greatest teachers and thinkers of both the past and present point out that much of what we call happiness or suffering arises in our own "internal" minds. If this is indeed true (and there is much evidence that it is), then our prodigious and costly efforts to defeat human suffering through "external" technology are doomed to failure. No doubt we can improve certain situations for limited periods of time, but can we generally and universally remove pain? Will it not arise in some other form just as it has done over the ages? If pain arises within, might not the solution to it also be within? The first step in answering this question is to begin to look within, both individually and collectively.

The Triumph of Quantity over Quality

Over the greater part of human history, religion has provided humanity with a sense of purpose (for better or worse) beyond the mundane. With the ascendancy of modern science over the last

400 years, a relatively brief period in the context of human civilization, religion has been in retreat and the sense of any intrinsic purpose, value, and quality in life has waned. This process has accelerated dramatically in the last twenty years with the seeming triumph of the Capitalist "Free Market." Increasingly, many social policies and traditionally moral decisions are now being determined by whether or not a particular area of concern/venture can make a monetary profit or at least survive within a "balanced budget."

Some of the brightest contemporary minds have pinpointed the birth of empirical science during the early part of the seventeenth century as a major turning point in modern history. L.L. Whyte writes:

> Where Aristotle had classified, Kepler and Galileo sought to measure . . . . The process of measurement was the one objectively reliable approach to the structure of nature and the numbers so obtained were the key to the order of nature. After 1600 mankind was thus in possession of a systematic method of research into those aspects of nature which were accessible to measurement. The centuries since 1600 may well be regarded as the age of quantity.

These developments, as Ken Wilber has pointed out, eroded not only the church's (and religion's) authority and credibility, but also the general notion of any intrinsic value or quality in everyday life. Increasingly what was "real" and of value came to be regarded as only that which we could see, touch, and measure. All else was dismissed by science as "unreal," "superstition," "only in the mind," etc.

The Christian churches, both Catholic and Protestant, had set themselves up for ridicule by the emerging scientific movement by insisting on a strictly literal (despite many revisions and re-interpretations over the centuries) rather than symbolic or mystical interpretation of the scriptures. This interpretation led them, among other things, to make unwarranted pronouncements on the nature of the physical universe. Martin Luther's associate, Philipp

Melanchton, who died in 1560, unequivocally rejected the notion of the earth revolving around the sun, based mainly on certain passages in the Bible. In 1576, the Spanish inquisitor Leon of Castro proclaimed, "Nothing may be changed that disagrees with the Latin edition of the Vulgate (St. Jerome's translation of the Bible), be it a single period, a single conclusion, or a single clause."

In 1613, Galileo made the historic claim that his newly invented telescope proved Copernicus was indeed correct in theorizing that the sun was the center of the universe. Galileo was promptly summoned before the Inquisition and commanded to retract his theory. When he refused, he was jailed indefinitely. Over the following centuries, succeeding scientific (measured and verified) discoveries regarding the nature of the universe, evolution, etc., have made it clear that the church was fighting a futile and losing battle when they strayed from their proper religious and spiritual sphere. The church has been so battered ever since it now seems to have lost its nerve in matters concerning science and technology and is reluctant to make any kind of critical statement. John Naisbitt observed in his book *High Tech, High Touch*:

> It took the Catholic Church almost 400 years to concede that Galileo was right and almost 150 years to accept the theory of human evolution, but it took them less than 10 years to accept controversial genetic therapies.

The notion of intrinsic value, quality, or goodness was simultaneously (but not consciously) eroded from within the church itself. The early scientists like Descartes and Newton were devout Christians and sought to make their religion stronger by making God more rational and scientific. Attempts were made to rid Christianity of mystery and awe. In the 1670s, Newton was writing, "'Tis the temper of the hot and superstitious part of mankind in matters of religion ever to be fond of mysteries and for that reason to like best what they understand least." By 1730,

English theologian Matthew Tindal was championing the cause of reason within religion:

> There's a religion of nature and reason written into the hearts of every one of us from the first creation, by which all mankind must judge of the truth of any institutional religion whatever.

By 1882, Friedrich Nietzsche had taken this line of thinking to its logical conclusion and was proclaiming that God was dead. Ken Wilber writes about the erosion of the notion of quality and its link with the rise of scientism:

> The old hierarchy of value and being was thereby ditched in favor of a hierarchy of number. Certain realms could no longer be said to be higher or more real or better than others. We might say that levels of significance were replaced by levels of magnification . . . .

Scientism: The New Religion

There is no doubt that science and measurement are extremely powerful and useful tools. When those espousing a scientific approach, however, declare that anything that science cannot (presently) measure is not "real," science is being applied far beyond its appropriate range, similar to the way religion had been taken beyond its proper boundaries by those using it to make pronouncements on the nature of the physical universe. Science in that respect then becomes "scientism," a new religion that spawns the same kind of unhealthy dependence, expectation, blind obedience, and exploitation found in certain old-fashioned religions.

Science at present fulfills many of the functions religion once did. We look, even literally pray, to science for prosperous times and salvation with the same reverence and trust we once bestowed on God and religion. Most people acknowledge that we face grave environmental, social, and health problems but are not worried

because they feel, "Science will come up with something." When
scientific, medical, and technological innovations are introduced,
we enthusiastically buy into them, rarely questioning the necessity
for or the safety of the product. We do not think of a product's
generalized impact on society because we have been trained to
look for only simple, single cause and effect, which marketers
expertly (if selectively) highlight for us. In the case of medicine,
our dependence on the seeming omniscient and omnipotent
medical and pharmaceutical establishments is exaggerated since
we only go to the doctor when something is already obviously
wrong and then expect a miraculous quick fix or magic pill. People
presently abuse themselves with food, alcohol, tobacco, drugs, and
reckless lifestyles and then expect medicine to not only return them
to health but to youthful good looks. All of this creates a victimlike
dependence and helplessness, which militate against taking personal
responsibility or preventative action.

The Dalai Lama warned:

> My concern is we are apt to overlook the limitations of
> science. In replacing religion as the final source of knowledge
> in popular estimation, science begins to look a bit like another
> religion itself.

Huston Smith in his book, *Forgotten Truth: The Common Vision
of the World's Religions*, explained how science, despite its limitations,
became the sole arbiter of "reality":

> Modern science only requires one ontological level, the
> physical. Within this level, it begins with matter that is
> perceptible, and to perceptible matter it in the end
> returns, for however far its hypotheses extend . . . . Itself
> occupying no more than a single ontological plane,
> science challenged by implication the notion that other
> planes exist. As its challenge was not effectively met, it
> swept the field.

Many scientists, for example, regard "consciousness" as nothing more than electrical currents and chemical reactions taking place within the physical brain. I took part in a web-cast roundtable dialogue to mark the first "World Day of Planetary Consciousness," and during our discussions, a professor of psychiatry and neuroscience straightforwardly confessed that the whole notion of a "global" or "planetary" consciousness just did not make much sense to her, given her field of study. Ken Wilber, in his *Sex, Ecology and Spirituality*, writes about the brain and consciousness thusly:

> The within or actual interior of the brain is not inside the brain. Inside the brain is just more brain physiology. Empirically examine the brain all you want with microscopes, EEG, etc., and you will still only have the insides of the brain . . . and not the interior or the within of the brain, which is depth or consciousness (and which you can find only by talking to me and interpreting what I say). The brain itself is exterior to consciousness, it is another (potential) form in consciousness . . . . Consciousness is not inside the brain and not outside of it either . . . and therefore moves wherever it likes without ever leaving the brain because it was never in the brain to begin with (and never apart from it either). How else explain, for example, the phenomenon of individual and group identity?

As a Qigong healer and teacher of Daoist and Buddhist mind-body disciplines, I run into scientism on a regular basis and have had an opportunity to observe it from the "front lines" for over 25 years. Initially, I set out to explain and demonstrate how the mind, emotions, energy (Qi), and physical body interact and how we could use this knowledge to better our physical and mental health and also transform our consciousness to become wiser and more compassionate human beings, capable of very efficient functioning in the everyday world. Being a former chartered accountant with extensive experience of different kinds of working environments, I felt I could explain these seemingly exotic matters in logical, everyday terms that ordinary "hardheaded" people could understand.

While I always knew my potential "market" would be small, I am still amazed how few people want to explore a perspective of life that makes logical sense of our postmodern confusion and that has been taught by the greatest teachers the world has produced. I think the numbers of people who are interested or curious are increasing, but there is a strong force which keeps most people locked into a basically "scientism" approach to life, even if re-cast in "alternative" or New Age spirituality terms. People still look for quick solutions to specific problems, avoiding any complexity or commitment; there is an attraction to "gadgets" and magic formulas; many consciously or subconsciously still look for signs of a savior or messiah, whether human, alien, or technological; the promise of easy youthfulness and prosperity is always a big seller.

Even when "non-conventional" or "traditional" methods and practices are embraced, they are often packaged and marketed in a conventional manner—specific benefits, glossy presentation, limited scope. Whenever there is money to be made, it is surprising how quickly the "establishment" often turns from scientific/logical scorn and dire warnings to sudden "research" and "evidence" to justify their leap on to the profit bandwagon. Eastern and traditional methods are being systematically pulled apart, packaged, and marketed. Some people see this as a sign of open-mindedness and progress. It is also commercialization, trivialization, and fragmentation. What remains missing and ignored in this rush to market is the elusive sense of wholeness, connectedness, and simplicity. This is difficult to measure, market, and cultivate but is the most precious ingredient of all because without it, we will continue to fragment as individuals and as a society.

The Costs of Free Market Morality

As we have seen, the momentum of science and scientism over the last 400 years have taken us away from a world with a sense of innate mystery, value, quality, and purpose towards one in which "reality" is increasingly seen in stark material and quantifiable terms. The present ascendancy of the Capitalist "Free Market" is another significant development along this line of thinking. Endeavor should be justified on the basis of whether there is a sufficient quantity-of-dollar reward, whatever the nature of the product or activity. Among the most noticeable examples of this development have been the widespread marketing of sex and sexuality as well as the social acceptance of lying and deception within advertising, marketing, politics, law etc.

While watching the TV news, my attention was caught by someone forcefully speaking in favor of President Bush's plan to aggressively pursue Arctic oil exploration in sensitive nature reserves and to construct more coal-fired and atomic energy power stations—despite the damaging effects of coal emissions on health and the environment, the problem of radioactive waste disposal, and the fact that America could save more oil through raising automotive efficiency than it could derive from drilling the Arctic. He bluntly stated that human interests were paramount and that if we needed more energy, we should not be deterred by damage to mere trees and the environment in general. The TV caption identified him as a representative of the Ayn Rand Institute, of which I was ignorant at that time, having been educated in England and Guyana.

I was determined to find out more about the Ayn Rand Institute because I was surprised that people still thought like that and moreover that their views were being featured on prime-time American TV (CNN). I visited the Ayn Rand Institute website and was intrigued to discover that several factors that I had previously identified as contributing to society's problems were actually the trumpeted foundation of Ayn Rand's philosophy, which she called "Objectivism."

I present hereunder a brief summary of "Objectivism" as taken from the website. Its metaphysics is "Objective Reality," epistemology is "Reason," ethics is "Self-interest," and politics is "Capitalism."

"Objective reality" means that:

> Reality, the external world, exists independent of man's
> consciousness, independent of any observer's knowledge,
> beliefs, feelings, desires or fears . . . Thus Objectivism rejects
> any belief in the supernatural—and any claim that
> individuals or groups create their own reality.

The summary of "Ethics" concludes:

> (Man) must work for his rational self-interest, with the
> achievement of his own happiness as the highest moral
> purpose of his life. Thus Objectivism rejects any form of
> altruism—the claim that morality consists in living for others
> or for society.

The political system that Ayn Rand advocates is *Laissez-faire*
Capitalism in which the only function of government is to protect
individual citizens from physical force. Objectivism rejects any
form of collectivism, such as fascism or socialism, and also the
notion of a "mixed economy," in which the government attempts
to regulate the economy and redistribute wealth.

Although some identify Ayn Rand with right-wing Republicans
and Conservatives, I think her views are shared by many in modern
society and, as such, deserve attention. I subsequently discovered
from a newspaper article that Alan Greenspan, longtime chairman
of the U.S. Federal Reserve Board and *de facto* pilot of the U.S.
economy under several Republican presidents as well as Democrat,
Bill Clinton, is not only a follower of Ayn Rand's philosophy but
was also a close personal friend. I was surprised at first, but when I
pondered the ramifications, I could more clearly understand many
of the dynamics apparent in America (and subsequently emanating
into the wider world).

The denial of cause and effect on the grounds that a direct link
is not "sufficiently" quantifiable is a product of "scientism" and is
prominent in offshoots like "Objectivism." This denial is illogical,

shortsighted, and extremely dangerous, because it cuts us off from the true consequences of our actions. It is even more dangerous because most people are not even aware that this denial exists since they are so steeped in scientism.

Right now, environmental damage and pollution caused by the "rational self-interest" of countless individuals are killing people, wiping out entire species of flora and fauna, and devastating the planet at an alarming rate. Those in big business and government who are disinclined to act, put forward Ayn Randian—type arguments—we should wait for more conclusive research; cause and effect cannot be pinned down to individual citizens, corporations or countries; we need less government not more; remedial action would hurt our "competitiveness," etc. George W. Bush not only put forward such arguments but also unilaterally withdrew America—by far the world's greatest per capita polluter—from the Kyoto Protocol on global warming, which had been signed by almost every country on the planet after years of difficult negotiations.

Professor Thomas Homer-Dixon, in his book, *The Ingenuity Gap*, described several of the dramatic environmental changes taking place around the planet. He pointed out that in the 1980s, scientists drilling deep into the pristine ice of Antarctica found remarkably consistent correlations over hundreds of thousands of years between carbon dioxide levels and global temperatures. He wrote:

> The Vostok ice cores suggest temperature will rise, and perhaps rise fast. And one thing is certain: with each incremental ton of carbon we emit from our cars, power plants and logging operations, we are producing, inexorably, an atmosphere that is significantly different from the one that influenced human civilizations in the past.

The projected carbon dioxide and temperature levels from the accompanying graph in his book take a startling vertical leap to the top of the page! Right now, the hole in the ozone layer has increased the risk of skin cancer globally. In parts of the world, people are cautioned not to go out into the sun without some sort of protection for more than a few minutes at a time. Property damage due to extreme weather has increased dramatically as has coastal flooding, which in time will threaten low-lying cities like Miami.

The denial of cause and effect using a simplistic pseudoscientific rationale damages not only the planet but also other human beings. When it suits our purposes, we play on human vanity, in particular the notion that we are modern, sophisticated, in-control, eminently rational beings. This idea is fairly close to that put forward by the Ayn Rand Institute—"Objectivism rejects any form of determinism, the belief that man is a victim of forces beyond his control (such as God, fate, upbringing, genes, or economic conditions)." When it comes to accepting responsibility, however, we suddenly discover some form of determinism and deny such matters are within the bounds of our control.

I agree it is unlikely that a single specific factor determines (in the sense of definitely causes) a specific kind of human behavior, but that does not mean that a factor cannot significantly influence one person's behavior or statistically influence the behavior of many people. With repetition over time and from different sources, the influence of specific factors can be greatly magnified. Think of the many ideas or practices that we once found abhorrent and crazy but are now "normal" because of our continued exposure to them especially through the popular media.

Those who make their living by influencing and predicting our behavior—politicians, marketing and media people, the entertainment industry, pollsters, etc.—not surprisingly promote the soothing and flattering notion that each person is objective and rationally able to choose. At the same time, however, those same people rely heavily on opinion polls, focus groups, etc., to tell them how most people or specific target groups will (predictably) react. Since there are proven ways of consistently swaying behavior (spin doctors, lifestyle ads, sound and video bites, "testimonials," pseudo-documentaries, etc.), then it would seem that the whole notion of the average person is rational and objective, is at best inconsistent and contradictory, and at worst, a lie used to facilitate the manipulation of mass opinions and attitudes.

A U.S. Federal Trade Commission report in 2000, ordered by President Bill Clinton after the Columbine High School massacre the previous year, discovered that R-rated "adult" electronic games, CDs, and videos were routinely and intentionally marketed to children as young as nine years old. Underage children were included in research screenings, and marketers targeted kids' websites, teenage hangouts, and even the Campfire Boys and Girls. The report found "a high correlation between exposure to media violence and aggressive, and at times, violent behavior."

After being threatened with regulatory legislation, eight of the country's top film producers offered a vaguely worded voluntary code concerning violent (but not sexual) material. They, however, stopped short of promising they would stop all marketing to children under 17 years old. They denied any responsibility for moral decay and said it was up to parents, not corporations, to monitor kids' viewing and listening habits. Jack Valenti, industry lobbyist and head of the Motion Picture Association of America, employing creatively obscure logic, indignantly declared, "If we are causing moral decay in this country, we ought to have an explosion in crime. The exact opposite is happening." It was a classic "sound bite" aimed to override serious and complex issues and probably seemed reasonable to many people.

It is a common urban joke to assert that "Advertising works, but not on me!" The sad part is that most people actually seem to believe this. The longer we maintain this arrogant yet misguided stance, however, the more we will be exploited by those who make a lucrative living out of influencing us and the further we will be deflected from straight-talking honesty. Surely the first step towards deeper Truth, or even a clearer perspective, is simple honesty.

Because we have managed to sever cause from effect (and therefore responsibility), traditional moral codes have been battered. Greed, lust, envy, theft, and even killing can be blamed on the anonymous "Market," "System," or "Society." All of these, however, have been created and sustained by our individual decisions—voting, purchasing, investing, etc. Behind anonymous corporations are people making decisions—managers, employees, and shareholders.

Many of the products on the Free Market are driven by the rationale and lure of the underlying American Dream—the idea that anyone can overcome the overwhelming odds, "make it," and flaunt it as a sign of being different and special.

There will always be individuals who will be held up as examples of having beaten the odds, but the vast majority will struggle in vain. In the U.S.A. and in the world at large, the gap between the rich and poor has been growing for the last 40 years, and this is becoming a significant destabilizing factor. Even in wealthy North American cities, it is becoming common to see people living on the streets, even in the depths of winter. The Organization for Economic Co-operation and Development conservatively estimates that the world's population will increase by 25 percent (to 7.5 billion) by 2020 with 4 billion people living in cities, many of them "monster" cities with 15-25 million or more, generating immense air and water pollution, together with mountains of garbage. Faith Birol, the head of the International Energy Agency, estimates that by 2020, the developing countries alone will have to build 30,000 new electric power plants to meet anticipated demand. This presumes there will be enough energy resources, which are estimated to peak around 2016.

All this misery and poverty is undoubtedly as much a product of Free Market Capitalism as its success stories. Thus, we in the West should not be surprised by the appearance of reactionary elements like terrorism and fundamentalism. They also are part of the system—where there is Yin, there is Yang; the blade of the sword has two edges.

Technology: The Future

Unless there is a drastic about-turn in attitude and approach, our world will continue to be shaped by the Science-Technology-Capitalism complex, just as it has been over the last few centuries.

The twenty-first-century technologies—robotics, genetics and nano-(molecular) technology—will transform our lives in ways it is difficult for us to even imagine. These technologies will not only be awesomely powerful but also will be capable of self-replication and will change the very notion of what it means to be "human." Many well-placed researchers are presently proceeding on the assumption that technological evolution and human evolution are one and the same! The present consensus of opinion is that this frenetic momentum will be difficult to stop since it is part of the established Free Market system, and these new technologies all have consumer applications. A radical change in direction will require radical changes in our individual and collective attitudes as well as in our systems including political, economic, legal and medical.

Some of the world's foremost robotics experts seriously regard future machines as spiritual beings and as our "mind children." To them, the evolution of technology is synonymous with the evolution of human beings. Dr. Ray Kurzweil, inventor of the Kurzweil Reading Machine for the blind and author of *The Age of Spiritual Machines: When Computers Exceed Human Intelligence*, writes:

> Technological evolution moves us inexorably closer to becoming like God. And the freeing of our thinking from the severe limitations of our biological form may be regarded as an essential spiritual quest. By the close of the next century, nonbiological (machine) intelligence will be ubiquitous. There will be few humans without some form of artificial intelligence.

Hans Moravec, founder of one of the world's largest robotics research programs at Carnegie Mellon University, writes in his book, *Robot: Mere Machine to Transcendent Mind*

> Biological species almost never survive encounters with superior competitors . . . .In a completely free marketplace,

superior robots would surely affect humans as North American placentals affected South American marsupials (and as humans have affected countless species). Robotic industries would compete vigorously among themselves for matter, energy, and space, incidentally driving their price beyond human reach. Unable to afford the necessities of life, biological humans would be squeezed out of existence.

In a subsequent article entitled, "Robots, Re-evolving Mind," published in December 2000, Moravec took his ideas a step further, elaborating on how and why robots will evolve quickly to surpass human beings and why, in his opinion, that is a good thing. Moravec wrote:

Computers have permeated everyday life and are worming their way into our gadgets, dwellings, clothes, even bodies . . . We seem to be re-evolving mind (in a fashion) at ten million times the original speed! . . . Barring cataclysms, I consider the development of intelligent machines a near-term inevitability . . . By performing better and cheaper, robots will displace humans from essential roles. Rather quickly, they could displace us from existence. I'm not as alarmed as many by the latter possibility, since I consider these future machines our progeny, "mind children" built in our image and likeness.

Moravec's "near-term inevitability" is perhaps a mere 30 years away, when computers will be a million times more powerful than today and approaching human-level computing as well as self-replication.

In addition to robotics, the twenty-first century will see the continued development of genetics, which has already come to popular attention through Dolly, the cloned sheep, and genetically modified or engineered foods, which are presently known as GMOs (genetically modified organisms). Fish genes have been inserted into strawberries, viruses into squash, bacterial genes into corn, etc.

Although current developments represent just the tip of the genetics iceberg, the still brief history of their introduction provides an (alarming) insight into the way corporations, often supported by cooperative government agencies, sell new technologies to the public, whether or not they want the new product.

Firstly, because there are no precedents (and therefore no regulations) and the application is ostensibly commercial rather than military, there is very little control on the initial introduction of a new product or technology. It usually takes time for any mistakes or unforeseen consequences to show up, which gives the seller a "honeymoon" window of opportunity to get their product into the market and reap profits.

Similar to the way that pharmaceutical companies give free samples of new drugs, funding and other incentives to doctors and hospitals, the major GMO innovators like Monsanto (which also manufactures pharmaceuticals) went to the source, the farmers, promising them huge profits through the new "designer" technology of the GMOs. Monsanto's Roundup Ready Soybeans, for instance, was supposed to resist not only insects but also the very popular Roundup weed killer, which was also a Monsanto product. Sensing ever greater profits, Monsanto purchased the rights to the "terminator" genetic technology, which prevents plants from reproducing—which would mean that farmers would have to keep on buying seeds from Monsanto.

The early attempts to market GMOs to the public on the grounds that the products were different and better (Flavr Savr tomato, etc.) were unsuccessful because the public was wary of them and were able to identify them. The industry, especially in the U.S. and Canada, then quickly switched to the opposite tactic— persuading the regulatory bodies that these crops were not "substantially different" from ordinary produce and therefore should not be subject to any special handling or regulation, including labeling. Government bodies looked favorably on GMOs probably because of the powerful farmers' lobby and because America, Canada, and Australia were in the forefront of GMO innovation, generating profits and taxes.

This second strategy worked exceedingly well with GMOs being shipped to market alongside and mixed in with unmodified products. GMOs appeared in supermarkets not only as fresh produce but in processed foods. It is estimated that in the U.S.A., GMOs had captured 60 percent of the market within 4 years of their introduction in the mid-'90s. The percentages in Canada were not far behind. Popular GMO crops included corn, canola, soy beans, and potatoes.

By 2000, however, persistent protests and lobbying by consumer activists, especially in Europe, were keeping "Frankenfoods" in the headlines, and the North American public was becoming incensed by their governments' stubborn refusal to legislate the labeling of GMOs as such. Government representatives were beginning to sound like industry lobbyists, and in Canada this impression was reinforced when it was revealed that the government had spent more than $280,000 to promote the use of Monsanto GMOs. As public resistance mounted, products were pulled from shelves, and farmers cut back on planting GMOs. Newspaper articles declared, "Tide is turning against genetically altered foods."

Just a year later, however, in June 2001, a *New York Times* article was declaring, "As biotech crops multiply, consumers get little choice." David Barboza wrote:

Despite persistent concerns about genetically modified crops, they are spreading so rapidly that it has become almost impossible for consumers to avoid them . . . More than 100 million acres of the world's most fertile farmland were planted with genetically modified crops last year, about 25 times as much as four years earlier. Wind-blown pollen, commingled seeds and black-market plantings have further extended these products of biotechnology into the far corners of the globe—perhaps irreversibly, according to food experts. Biotech industry officials believe the game is nearly won.

The next big play in the genetics game—and it might be the

end game—is of course its application to human beings. As with GMOs, the public is struggling to grasp even the broad possibilities and implications of IGM (inheritable genetic modification) and cloning, while actual research and marketing strategies are going ahead at breakneck competitive speed. Much of this research is clandestine because current opinion polls suggest the public is "not ready" for cloning. In early 2001, American scientists' revelation of ANDi, the first genetically modified monkey, surprised many of their colleagues. Dr. Christopher Exley, a research fellow at Keele University in England, commented: "Without a doubt, all the necessary checks and balances are not in place, but I'm not sure that we know exactly what we need to do either . . . we must assume lots of other things like this are going on."

Genetic testing of embryos for certain types of cancer is already taking place. It is to be expected (given the track record of technological innovation and implementation) that this testing will be extended to other serious diseases, then less serious diseases and eventually to genetic traits, i.e., testing with the object of producing designer babies. Judging from the eagerness of people to "improve" themselves through radical cosmetic surgery, designer babies are not really a stretch of the imagination.

A *Time Magazine* article by Nancy Gibbs in February 2001 reported that biotechnology specialists expect the birth of the first human clone within just a few years. She writes:

> At that moment, at least two things will happen—one private and one public. The meaning of what it is to be human—which until now has involved, at the very least, the mysterious melding of two different people's DNA—will shift forever, along with our understanding of the relationships between parents and children, means and ends, ends and beginnings. And as a result, the conversation that has occupied scientists and ethicists for years, about how much men should mess with nature when it comes to reproduction, will drop onto every kitchen table, every pulpit, every politician's desk.

The implications of and potential problems with cloning and genetic manipulation are numerous, disturbing and far reaching and should be discussed at all levels right now while there is still time to make choices. Unfortunately, however, many people, even within positions of influence, do not understand the technical implications and, as we have seen, are already confused about human value and meaning. Moreover, we seem to be always more preoccupied with the current state of our economy, whether good or bad.

As if all of this is not already overwhelming, scientists are developing a third new branch of technology, which is presently known as "nanotechnology." Nanotechnology is a hybrid of chemistry and engineering that holds out the promise of enabling us to manipulate matter at the atomic and molecular levels. Supporters of this technology are making claims of utopian abundance—that it would enable us to cheaply manufacture or replicate any known substance, conquer disease, and completely control our physical world. Some see the possibility, for instance, of creating submicroscopic, self-replicating robots that we could introduce into our bodies by swallowing them in pill form for various purposes—to fight diseases, program our bodies, or merely enjoy pleasurable virtual experiences.

As usual, however, there is another side. These powerful new technologies may give rise to overwhelming complications and mutations we do not anticipate or may simply be used against us by those with destructive intentions—terrorists, the criminally insane, etc. What better way to bring down a greedy and arrogant technology-based society than by turning its own technology against it? In the near future, technologies will be so powerful one person with a laptop computer will be able to cause widespread disaster. Indeed, it is possible right now.

Ironically, one of those presently sounding the loudest warnings about twenty-first-century technologies is a prominent technology insider. Bill Joy, cofounder and chief scientist of Sun Microsystems and co-chair of the presidential commission on the future of IT research, wrote a lengthy article for *Wired* magazine entitled, "Why the future doesn't need us." He subsequently traveled across North America to spread his message of concern. Alarmed by the visions of people like Kurzweil, Moravec, and Theodore Kaczynski (The Unabomber), he wonders why others are not afraid and why there is no discussion of these amazing new technologies:

> Why weren't other people more concerned about these nightmarish scenarios? Part of the answer certainly lies in our attitude toward the new—in our bias toward instant familiarity and unquestioning acceptance. Accustomed to living with almost routine scientific breakthroughs, we have yet to come to terms with the fact that the most compelling 21st century technologies—robotics, genetic engineering, and nanotechnology—pose a different threat than the technologies that have come before. Specifically robots, engineered organisms, and nanobots share a dangerous amplifying factor: they can self-replicate. A bomb is blown up only once—but one bot can become many and quickly get out of control.

Joy warns that nanotechnology can be easily used for military purposes, targeting specific geographic areas or genetically distinct groups of people. He points out that nanotechnology could possibly pose a threat to the entire planet, quoting from Eric Drexler's *The Engines of Creation*:

> Plants with "leaves" no more efficient than today's solar cells could out-compete real plants, crowding the biosphere with an inedible foliage. Tough omnivorous "bacteria" could out-compete real bacteria. They could spread like blowing pollen, replicate swiftly and reduce the biosphere to dust in a matter of days.

Fundamentalism, New Age Spirituality, and Postmodernism

Several prominent thinkers and writers, including Matthew Fox, Jean Houston, and Ervin Laszlo, have pointed to the first decade of this new millennium as a crucial one-one of critical "Breakdown" or "Breakthrough," as Laszlo describes it. The latter requires an unprecedented quantum leap in human consciousness. The call for urgent change is coming simultaneously from many important areas of our lives—environmentalists warning about the fragile health of the planet; economists and politicians warning about the volatility of the poverty gap; technology insiders and ethicists warning about the need to control scientific and technological innovation; civil libertarians and anti-globalists warning about the power of multinational corporations and government; spiritual leaders calling for peace, justice, compassion, and attention to our inner, spiritual life.

Many of these voices also independently report a puzzling deafness or lack of response to their warnings within their respective areas of concern. This is consistent with polls, which have found that although Americans acknowledge that there are real problems with the environment, terrorism, etc.,. their main ongoing concern and expectation is to retain their own (high) standard of living. The American presidential election of 2000 was telling in this respect. Voters, enjoying unprecedented prosperity, decided to invest massive budget surpluses in relatively small tax rebates for themselves rather than begin tackling problems like the environment, schools, health care, poverty, etc. They voted for a "big business" Republican presidential candidate who would preserve the "American Way" of consumerism and cheap energy at any cost, even in the face of growing global opposition.

I think that much of this inertia is due to the overwhelming complexity and pressure of modern society. People, after a hard day's work, do not have the energy to inquire and would not know where to start or whom to believe. Most just want to sit in front of the TV and numb themselves. In the absence of any clear understanding or choice, many profess to be generally "positive" and "optimistic," which is a continuation of the good/evil, light/dark duality that has long dominated Western religion and culture. In many ways, being optimistic is good, but it is not conducive to objective examination and inquiry. Life is always changing and demands specific responses, which rarely fall conveniently into our simplistic "positive/negative" or "good/bad" slots. No response is in itself a response.

As we have seen, most people are techno-optimists—followers of scientism, who expect science and technology to come up with endless miracle solutions. Other kinds of optimists, who realize that a change in human behavior is necessary, see signs of spiritual renewal or even a consciousness breakthrough, citing signs of spirituality all over the world—New Age spirituality, the interfaith movement, Christian, Islamic and Jewish fundamentalism, the ecological movement, the worldwide spread of Eastern spiritual traditions like Buddhism, Hinduism and Daoism, and the many forms of Shamanism, especially Native American.

I would agree that all of these are indeed signs of spiritual activity and probably that most of them are a reaction to the denial and, in some cases, suppression of inner spiritual life and qualities like caring, compassion, equilibrium, balance, quietude, etc. I am not convinced, however, that they all signal a quantum leap forward in human consciousness since some of them are just a reconfiguration of what we already practice (which is not working) while others are a retrogressive desire to return to feudal values.

Probably the most obvious (and disturbing) sign of religious activity is "fundamentalism" of any ilk—mostly Muslim, Christian, Jewish, and recently Hindu in India. In the name of the one true God or religion, fundamentalists have assassinated abortionists, political leaders, military personnel, and many thousands of ordinary citizens.

One of the main problems with fundamentalism (and indeed with Western Abrahamic religion generally) is that each sect claims that God is on its side in the battle between "good" and "evil" and that you are either a "believer" or "non-believer." This leaves a lot of people on the "wrong" side. The most famous example of fundamentalist violence so far is the September 11 attack, which was carried out by terrorists led by Osama bin Laden and his al-Qaeda group. It is interesting that in one of his first speeches after the attacks, President George W. Bush, a Christian of fundamentalist leanings, avowed to conduct a "crusade" against the terrorists. The original Crusades, which began in the twelfth century CE and lasted over a hundred bloody years, was as an attempt by European Christians to liberate the Holy Lands (now Israel) in Palestine from Muslim control. Bush repeatedly spoke of "a conflict between good and evil" and reassured his people that "God is not neutral" and was on America's side.

Bin Laden, in his first speech after the attacks, also emphasized the religious component of the conflict in terms strikingly similar to Bush's:

> These events have divided the whole world into two sides—
> the side of the believers and the side of infidels, may God
> keep you away from them. Every Muslim has to rush to
> make his religion victorious. The winds of faith have come.
> The winds of change have come to eradicate oppression
> from the island of Muhammad.

Many fundamentalists unequivocally reject the trappings and rationale of modern society and seek to go back in time to seemingly simpler days while others see the unfolding of specific prophesies. Several biblical scholars discern signs of the prophesized "end times." We are beginning to hear cries of "Crusade" and "Jihad" that originated nearly a thousand years ago. In her *The Battle for God*, best-selling religious author and scholar, Karen Armstrong, writes about the rise of fundamentalism:

> In the late 1970s, fundamentalists began to rebel against
> this secular hegemony and started to wrest religion out of its
> marginal position and back to centre stage. In this, at least,
> they have enjoyed remarkable success. Religion has once
> again become a force that no government can safely
> ignore . . . . Fundamentalists do not regard this battle as a
> conventional political struggle, but experience it as a cosmic
> war between the forces of good and evil.

I see fundamentalism as an extreme and literal form of popular religion. In many ways, it is more honest than popular religion because it does not try to hide its claims of exclusivity and its logical contradictions, but celebrates them in a plain and aggressive manner. I do not think that either fundamentalism or popular religion is the vehicle to take us safely into the future because they are both rigid and conducive to conflict, which is very dangerous given the devastating weapons at our present disposal and being developed for the future. Belief is undoubtedly powerful, but it leaves no room for the belief of others, taking us down the well-trod road of the "saved" and the "damned," except sometimes it is difficult to tell who is who. Popular religion will be discussed at greater length in chapter three. Although I will not discuss fundamentalism further, I acknowledge it as an extremely powerful force with which we must all reckon. It has the considerable appeal of being simplistic and of enabling us to vent our anger and frustrations on a visible, "evil" enemy.

Another high-profile sign of spiritual activity is "New Age" spirituality. Its name is derived from the belief or conviction that humanity, transported by the movement of planetary energies, is entering a new astrological age, wherein ever-greater light, wisdom, love, spirituality, and harmony will prevail. Many proponents of this theory feel that all we have to do is to stay positive and go along for the ride. New Age spirituality consists of a wide spectrum of eclectic practices, including variations of popular religion, shamanism, pop-psychology, psychotherapy, sub-atomic physics, astrology, psychics, mediums, crystals, pendulums, alternative healing, and extraordinary beings including angels, inter-planetary aliens, nature spirits, and ghosts from the past, reaching back to ancient Egypt and fabled Atlantis.

I think New Age spirituality is indeed a movement towards higher consciousness, in particular the psychic level, but in its present form lacks the focus and urgency to dramatically impact everyday life. It is a colorful mixture of genuine spiritual work, charlatanism, narcissism, over-idealism (many New Agers are old Hippie Flower Children in a new guise), and messianic cults. It is postmodern in the sense that all the items in this mixed bag tend to be viewed as equal in quality and value, whether sublime or ridiculous.

Irrespective of where we stand on the spiritual spectrum, there are two matters, which should be of universal urgency. The first is the need for a greater sense of human value, caring, sharing, and integration in our society. The second is that we are facing crucial decisions that will impact on the fundamental quality of our lives and perhaps the survival of humanity as we know it. Even if we are indeed entering a New Age, we cannot afford to be complacent since the law of cause and effect always applies. We can possibly bomb, poison, or mutate ourselves to the point of extinction for many hundreds of years and still belatedly settle into our new astrological role. Most of us think in terms of hours, days, months, and years. That is the time frame for righting both our individual and collective lives, not in another thousand years. It is doubtful that the millions who are presently dying of disease, starvation, and senseless military conflicts are comforted by the fact that we may be entering a New Age.

For a renewed and more evolved form of spirituality to take root and blossom, we need within the global spiritual community a common vision and voice. How can the different established religions advise the person in the street, much less politicians, lawyers, soldiers, doctors, business people, and scientists about spiritual and human values—compassion, harmony, oneness, etc.— if they still cannot agree among themselves?

Ironically, one of the obstacles to transcending our differences is the current well-meaning, relatively sophisticated, and politically correct conviction that all differing perspectives should be given equal weight. According to this stance, prevalent in academia and among the intelligentsia, differences are fine, and all we need is tolerance and discussion. Unfortunately, nothing gets decided or resolved since no one wants to be politically incorrect and say that something is better than another. The intelligentsia, artists, and spiritual leaders have failed to provide the vision and leadership expected of them, since they have largely frozen themselves into inaction. Meanwhile, others with much baser motives and sensibilities determine our collective destiny. In other words, while intellectuals quibble over words, the strong prey on the weak. The seriousness of this neglect increases apace with the burgeoning, uncontrolled power of our technologies.

This perspective, increasingly labeled "postmodern," has been slowly emerging over the last few decades but blossomed in the late '80s and early '90s. It correctly recognizes the fact that since no perspective is final (since it is conditioned) and that we are all human beings, we should therefore include and respect all cultures and viewpoints. We should not discriminate against Blacks, Muslims, women, homosexuals, natives, Asians, Jews, the handicapped, the overweight, etc. So far, so good.

The problem is that respect for other viewpoints and for basic human rights has somehow been simplistically condensed into a new dogma wherein all viewpoints are deemed equal. Many people do not seem to discern much difference between these two stances and think those pointing it out are being unnecessarily pedantic and negative or just ignorant and reactionary—old-fashioned male chauvinists and "red necks."

If all perspectives are equal, then there is nothing any more valuable or qualitatively better than anything else, which lands us back at pretty much the same position as that held by scientism— no inherent quality or "other worldliness," just numbers, measurement, dollars, brute force, and a universe of colliding objects. This is ironic, since many people aspiring to multiculturalism see themselves as a counterforce to the materialistic attitudes currently associated with science and technology.

If we do not recognize the fact that certain perspectives may be qualitatively better than others or may represent a higher level of consciousness, then we are in big trouble. If all perspectives are indeed equal, then it also follows that no perspective has any special value. This not only blocks the pursuit of spiritual evolution, but the very notion of it. It makes us reluctant to make moral decisions (lest we offend or discriminate), and those we do make tend to be inconsistent since we are confused—picking at random or out of reaction. Life begins to lose meaning since there is no real reason to work at anything (to qualitatively improve)—a relationship, the community, the environment, a job, art, spirituality, etc. If others treat your efforts on par with everyone else's, no matter how stupid, brutish, or even insane those might be, then what is the point of even trying?

Furthermore, if we shy away from moral decisions (and we seem to be, since we are increasingly turning them over to the anonymous "market"), then those who are decisive and forceful, regardless of their motives, will make our decisions for us and shape the future. We will have given away our power to act, and our sense of moral superiority will be meaningless.

Ken Wilber writes about the emergence of postmodernism in the early '90s in his book, *A Theory of Everything*:

> Extreme postmodernism and the green meme (a certain level of consciousness) had completely invaded academia . . . It claimed that all truth is culturally situated (except its own truth, which is true for all cultures); it claimed there were no transcendental truths (except its own pronouncements, which transcend specific contexts); it claimed that all hierarchies or value rankings are oppressive and marginalizing (except its own value ranking, which is superior to the alternatives); it claimed that there were no universal truths (except its own pluralism).

The Antidote: Spirituality beyond Belief

The radical shift in human behavior and attitude required to cope with our collective problems is well beyond routine choices of Republican or Democrat, more or less taxes, more or less military spending or aid, more or less conventional religion, etc. It requires a leap in consciousness to bridge the gap between our own evolution as human beings and the advanced capabilities of our technology, which we have (unsuccessfully) tried to apply as a cure-all, including those problems that have resulted from human conflict and ignorance. Used inappropriately, technology can in turn create new problems and complications of immense proportions.

As a brief example of the above process, the splitting of the atom initially gave rise to hopes of several "ultimate solutions", including the ultimate weapon and the ultimate, cheap, clean and limitless energy source. The first hope was dashed as soon as the USSR predictably built their own atomic bomb, propelling us into a nuclear arms race, which still haunts us. Nuclear energy proved to be neither cheap nor clean. No one has yet worked out a satisfactory solution for safeguarding nuclear waste (dangerous for one hundred thousand years), for preventing accidents like Chernobyl or deliberate acts of sabotage, which have been made more likely through the widespread commercial export of nuclear technology. Even if safeguards are put in place, they have to be maintained over the long-term. The fall of the former USSR should be a warning in this regard. All of these complications were eminently foreseeable and the ensuing problems are thus part of the real cost of using nuclear technology, not just bad luck as some would have us think. It takes a lot of ingenuity to build a nuclear bomb or reactor but none to press a trigger button or make a stupid political, military or commercial decision concerning its usage.

Professor Homer-Dixon, a renowned political scientist, argues in his book, *The Ingenuity Gap*, that our "social ingenuity" is dangerously lagging behind our "technical ingenuity," and as a consequence, society is already too complex for us to handle. He explains:

> Technical ingenuity helps us solve problems in the physical world—such as requirements for shelter, food and transportation. Social ingenuity helps us meet the challenges we face in our social world. It helps us arrange our economic, political and social affairs and design our public and private institutions to achieve the level of well-being we want.

Prominent information technology insider, Bill Joy, warns that the twenty-first-century technologies pose an unprecedented threat to humanity because of their power and because they are basically uncontrolled and misunderstood. In his article entitled, "Why the future doesn't need us," he also calls for a "new ethical basis":

> A technological approach to Eternity—near immortality through robotics—may not be the most desirable utopia and its pursuit brings clear dangers . . . . Where can we look for a new ethical basis to set our course? I have found the ideas in the book *Ethics for the New Millennium* by the Dalai Lama to be very helpful . . . (he) argues that the most important thing is for us to conduct our lives with love and compassion for others and that our societies need to develop a stronger notion of universal responsibility and of our interdependency.

Best-selling author, social forecaster, corporate consultant, and sometime presidential adviser John Naisbitt, in his book, *High Tech, High Touch,* was deeply troubled by the unexpected findings of his own research into our future. He writes:

> Intoxicated by technology's seductive pleasures and promises, we turn our backs to technology's consequences and wonder why the future seems unpredictable . . . . We grant technology a special status, as if it's a natural law, an inalienable right . . . . This Intoxicated Zone is spiritually empty, dissatisfying, dangerous and impossible to climb out of unless we recognize that we're in it.

Throughout his book, Naisbitt stresses the need for a dialogue between politicians, scientists, economists, and especially theologians with a view to bringing more profound direction, purpose, and meaning to technological innovation:

> Even bioethicists see theologians as key participants in the process because they grapple with more fundamental questions of our humanity and less with the procedural or legal aspects of our new technologies.

Although the above authors and many others stress the need for a major change in human behavior—in effect a qualitative shift in consciousness or spiritual development—they do not suggest how this might occur. The "new ethics" or greater "social ingenuity" must be able to handle complexity, overcome divisions and conflict, discern in a rapidly changing environment what to let go and what to retain (i.e., make accurate subjective, value judgments), be capable of global perspective and responsibility, and perceive interconnectedness and subtle cause and effect in life.

The main purpose of this book is to suggest that the way towards such a consciousness shift (and beyond) has already been explained by the world's great spiritual teachers, within most of the world's great cultures and religions. Thus a spiritual common ground already exists, but it is little recognized, even by most of the current representatives of the world's popular religions. It is hidden in plain view.

This type of spirituality, which has existed for millennia, is variously termed Mystic, Metaphysical or Perennial/Ageless Wisdom spirituality. Unlike popular religion, which advocates belief and moral rules, backed by the promise and threat of heaven and hell, Ageless Wisdom teaches profound self-inquiry that leads to self-transformation. Rather than merely praying to God, we can experience the divine within ourselves and recognize the divine in all beings. Moral action springs not from fear or guilt but from being directly aware of the (divine) interconnectedness of all manifestation.

Ken Wilber, in his book, *One Taste*, pointed out that religion has historically fulfilled two functions:

> One, it acts as a way of creating meaning for the separate self: it offers myths and stories and narratives and rituals and revivals that taken together, help the separate self make sense of and endure the slings and arrows of outrageous fortune. This function of religion does not usually change the level of consciousness in a person . . . .

> Two, religion has also served—in a usually very, very small minority—the function of radical transformation and liberation. This function does not fortify the separate self, but utterly shatters it.

Huston Smith in his widely acclaimed *The World's Religions* describes religion in its widest sense as "life woven around a people's ultimate concerns," which are mostly mundane. Religion in its narrower sense (i.e., practiced by a minority) is "a concern to align humanity with the transcendental ground of its existence." Knowledge of the latter would be particularly apt right now as we prepare to tamper with our own evolution.

Transformational spirituality brings us both clarity of action (wisdom) and compassion since our underlying oneness becomes a reality, rather than a distant ideal. Since we would respond to life moment by unique moment, there would be no need for rigid and divisive belief systems, with their inevitable clash of believers and non-believers.

The Ageless Wisdom belongs to the whole of humanity, not just a chosen few. Alan Watts, former Anglican priest, doctor of divinity, and pioneering interpreter of Eastern philosophy, wrote in his book, *The Supreme Identity*, as early as 1950:

> Metaphysicians of the Christian tradition—pseudo-Dionysius, Eckhart, Albert the Great—teach essentially the same doctrine as Shankara and the Upanishads, and they in turn the same as Chinese Daoism and the Sufis of Islam. Add to this the corroborative support of the thousands who are more strictly mystics, and we have the most impressively unanimous body of teaching in the world.

The renowned author, Aldous Huxley, also stressed the universality and profundity of the Perennial Wisdom philosophy:

> Under all this confusion of tongues and myths, of local histories and particularist doctrines, there remains the Highest

Common Factor, which is the Perennial Philosophy in its pure state. This final purity can never be expressed by any verbal statement . . . . It is only in the act of contemplation, when words and even personality are transcended, that the pure state of the Perennial Philosophy can actually be known.

Perhaps the time has come for religion in the sense of personal transformation and liberation to enter more into the mainstream consciousness . . . for our internal human evolution to begin catching up with our technological prowess.

The first step would be to bring the knowledge of Ageless Wisdom spirituality to popular attention. In order to do this we must put aside both political correctness and religious taboos. It seems an unspoken rule on TV that you cannot push further once a person invokes the sacred truth of his or her "holy book" or scriptures. We fear the return of religious and racial bigotry, and so we back off. In fact, religious and racial bigotry never really went away but only became subtler, often hiding behind the cover of political correctness. Religious beliefs are the source of many of the conflicts within individual societies and in the world at large. We cannot resolve the conflicts they generate if we are not allowed to fully discuss them.

One of the rare times that religion became a mass media prime-time topic was immediately after the September 11 terrorist attacks. People all over the world, and especially in America, looked for deeper meaning and value; they spontaneously reached out to people of other religions. There was, however, no political or religious leadership to further and encourage this unique outpouring of goodwill and inquiry. People eventually determined to go back to their own separate religious roots. Most media discussions of religion feature only Judaism, Christianity, and Islam, which are in fact all part of the same (Western, Abrahamic) religion. To confuse matters even further, Islam is often incorrectly described as an "eastern" religion, while Hinduism and Buddhism are mostly ignored.

In his *Forgotten Truth*, Huston Smith warns, "The absence of a model for the world is the deepest definition of postmodernism and the confusion of our times. The two come close to being the same thing." The Ageless Wisdom is the foundation of such a model.

CHAPTER 2

THE HIDDEN EFFECTS OF TECHNOLOGY

Technology Is Not Neutral

As we saw in the previous chapter, the scientism mindset has conditioned us to approach and conduct life as a glorified scientific experiment—how best to study and manipulate the collection of physical objects "out there" in the external world for our personal benefit. In this process, we have also tended to think of the tools we use for manipulation as neutral objects, not dissimilar from the way that our far distant ancestors probably regarded rocks, branches, vines, etc. This attitude is evident in the slogan and rallying cry of the extremely powerful gun lobby in the U.S.A.—"Guns don't kill, people do."

Over 2,500 years ago, the Buddha pointed out that external objects were not separate from our internal minds. Internal "mind factors" not only cause different people to perceive the same external object differently, but also create much of the external world. Thus, for example, a slab of wood resting on two rocks may not be just a collection of physical objects but may serve the many purposes of what we now call a "table." Its creation may fulfill both functional and aesthetic requirements, and in that sense, is a product of mind.

In our present Information Age, it is absurd, but common nevertheless, to continue thinking of our technological tools as neutral. Peter Hershock, in his book, *Reinventing the Wheel: A Buddhist Response to the Information Age*, makes a distinction between "tools" and "technologies," pointing out that technologies now determine the movement of labor, resources, and capital. In the following passage, he uses television as an example:

> Seen as a tool, a television is something we can put away in the closet or disassemble for parts . . . by contrast, seen as technology, television—the distance transmission and reception of visual and auditory information—marks a significant and unique change in how we do things. Specifically, it transforms how we communicate with and entertain one another. It involves not just the cameras, transmitters and satellites and cables needed to electronically mediate our experience, but the factories that build these, the people working in those factories and the families they support, the producers and directors of the programs offered us, the editors and set builders, the reporters and advertisers. Involved as well are the conversations we have about soap opera characters, the music videos our teenagers consume with almost religious fervor, the toys modeled after TV puppets that we buy for our toddlers and the way these change the patterns of our play.

Reconsidering the slogan, "Guns don't kill, people do" in a similar light, it is obvious that tremendous amounts of expertise, history, planning, not to mention profit, are represented by the modern hand gun, rifle, shotgun, or automatic weapon. These weapons may not hunt down prey by themselves (as yet), but they have been designed to kill with great efficiency, and in many cases, they have been specifically designed to kill human beings. Yes, people will probably continue killing each other, but it is more difficult to kill another person armed with only a kitchen knife or baseball bat, much less go on a murderous rampage.

Social forecaster and corporate consultant John Naisbitt, while researching trends for his 1999 book, *High Tech, High Touch*, reached the conclusion that technology, far from being neutral, exhibited several marked characteristics:

> After scores of interviews with cultural leaders in business and arts, with academics and the theologians, and after careful examination of our own lives, we discovered a handful of clear symptoms that indicate an unsettling diagnosis of our way of life. The symptoms reveal our society to be a *Technologically Intoxicated Zone*, one defined by the complicated and often paradoxical relationship between technology and our search for meaning. The symptoms of a *Technologically Intoxicated Zone* are:

1. We favor the quick fix, from religion to nutrition.
2. We fear and worship technology.
3. We blur the distinction between real and fake.
4. We accept violence as normal.
5. We love technology as a toy.
6. We live our lives distanced and distracted.

Naisbitt concluded that a dialogue between scientists, politicians, etc., and theologians was urgently needed in order to bring purpose and meaning back into our lives. He was especially alarmed by the implications of uncontrolled genetics research. In this chapter, we will examine some of the general effects of technology, including Naisbitt's theories.

Is Reality Obvious?

The common view of reality more or less conforms to Ayn Rand's Objectivism. We see ourselves as rational beings, able to discern "objective reality" out there in the external world. This reality is regarded as existing independently of us (the observer) and has little or no impact on our ability to observe it. This world view or paradigm of an obvious, objective reality that can be reliably mapped has also been called "representational," "modern," "mechanistic," "Newtonian," etc.

Although we, as a society, pride ourselves on being logical and scientific, we have held on to the above view despite amazing advances in physics over the last century, which suggest that the actual dynamics of the universe are much more complex and interrelated. Many modern theories are built on the genius of Albert Einstein. The renowned contemporary physicist, David Bohm, describes our universe in very different terms from the Newtonian model:

> One is led to a new notion of unbroken wholeness which denies the classical idea of analyzability of the world into separately and independently existing parts . . . the inseparable quantum interconnectedness of the whole universe is the fundamental reality, and the relatively independently behaving parts are merely particular and contingent forms within this whole.

For millennia, the Mystic and Perennial Wisdom traditions have focused on the internal world, recognizing that much of our experience of "external reality" is actually conditioned by our own internal dynamics. If we are not aware of these dynamics, then we cannot detect our own biases and distortions. Moreover, since Spirit is the ground of all being, we can experience Spirit much more directly, fully, and consistently by transforming our consciousness to higher levels. We can do this by stripping away our illusions and distortions until we attain the clarity of "enlightenment." Buddhist meditation master Dhiravamsa writes in his book, *The Way of Non-attachment*:

> In Buddhism we are concerned with the man who is not just a man, and so we come to his real nature . . . First of all we have to put away the concept of a man usually accepted by society, we have to stop allowing accepted descriptions and explanations . . . In order to see man clearly, face to face,

we have to turn our attention inward and watch ourselves closely. We shall see the relationships existing within ourselves; how we relate to our thoughts, our feelings, sensations, perceptions, attitudes, tendencies and consciousness. Whenever we come into contact with an object, a situation or an experience, we form some kind of relationship with it which affects our behaviour.

Ken Wilber, in his innovative "Four Quadrants" theory, makes a distinction not only between the subjective and objective views of reality but also between the individual and collective. In the following passages, excerpted from his *Brief History of Everything*, he describes how he came upon his discovery. "Holarchies" (in the quote below) is Koestler's term for hierarchies, which in virtually all growth processes consist of "holons"—wholes that become parts of new, more complex wholes, e.g., atoms to cells to organisms:

> I started making lists of all these holarchical maps— conventional and new age, Eastern and Western, premodern and modern and postmodern—everything from systems theory to the Great Chain of Being, from the Buddhist vijnanas to Paiget, Marx, Kohlberg, the Vedantic koshas, Loevinger, Maslow, Lenski, Kaballah and so on . . .

> It dawned on me that there were actually four different types of holarchies . . . dealing with the inside and outside of a holon, in both its individual and collective forms—and that gives us four quadrants.

Wilber diagrammatically depicted his four quadrants as the result of two lines intersecting at right angles. Anything to the left of the vertical line represents looking at life from within or in other words, subjectively. To the right is an objective view of reality, as in a scientific experiment. Anything above the horizontal line relates to the individual and anything below the line relates to the collective. In each of the four quadrants, greater distance from the central point represents greater holarchy, complexity, and evolution. All four quadrants or perspectives of reality are interconnected and affect each other as Wilber explains below:

> An individual thought actually has at least these four facets, these four aspects—intentional, behavioural, cultural and social. And around the circle we go: the social system will have a strong influence on the cultural world view, which will set limits to the individual thoughts that I can have, which will register in the brain physiology. And you can go round the circle in any direction you want. The quadrants are all interwoven.

The scientism that we have been discussing so far in this book can be generally explained in Wilberian terms as the dominance of the external, right-hand quadrants (both individual and collective) over the internal, subjective left-hand quadrants. Homer-Dixon described it as our advanced "technical ingenuity" not being matched by equivalent "social ingenuity." It should be noted that the objective, right-hand quadrants' view of reality is not wrong, merely incomplete.

The Impact of Media, Culture, and Society

Rapid technological advances in communications, corporate concentration and the common but erroneous assumption that we as individuals are not really affected by the media, have resulted in major social changes slipping past our democratic review process. In other words, unmonitored forces, many of which are being consciously directed by small, special interest groups, are rapidly transforming our lives and our planet.

To even novice students of history, psychology, etc., it is obvious that the individual has throughout history been influenced by his or her culture and social environment. We can regard "culture" as how those around us think and act. The effect is stronger if there is a strong group identity reinforced by emotional ties. Traditionally, this has meant family, friends, tribe, race, country, and religion, bolstered by sacred beliefs, legend, history, etc. More recently, other cultural influences have arisen—schools, universities, and especially the mass media/ entertainment industries.

The second major collective influence on the individual is the external environment, including the social systems within which we have to live and function—technological, medical, economic, corporate, legal, political, educational, etc. With the rapid acceleration of technological innovation, especially within the last fifty years, this "quadrant" of society is exerting a tremendous amount of influence on both individuals and culture. Consider, for example, the life style changes engendered just by TV, cell phones and computers.

For the first time in human history, Scientism and Free Market capitalism have brought together the technical ability to broadcast words and images globally with the corporate power to effectively control the content of those broadcasts. Some multinational corporations not only have bigger budgets than many sovereign nations but also wield more political power. These corporations often evade accountability by threatening to shift (or actually shifting) their centers of operations to countries that will afford them shelter and less scrupulous regulation. Corporations also fund much scientific and technological research and to that extent are aggressively shaping our future, without any popular input or consultation. For example, if your phone or cable TV companies want to introduce new (more expensive) technical systems, there is nothing you can do about it apart from not using phones or having TV. Since the openly declared motivation of most corporations is profit and self-interest, wider social impacts are largely ignored or denied.

The explosion in communications technology has enabled individuals, corporations, and governments to directly shape public opinion on an unprecedented scale. Corporations like AOL-Time Warner, Disney, and News Corp. (Rupert Murdoch) not only control the media through which information and entertainment is delivered—newspapers, magazines, books, films, cable TV, the

Internet, music videos, CDs, DVDs, etc.—but the actual content. Even though these entities compete with each other, because the bottom line is profit, standards and values tend to give way to sensationalism and sink down to the lowest common denominator. We are offered a lot of superficial choice and variety, but the product is essentially the same, regardless of the specific provider. Rapid turnover and mass consumption of mediocrity mean massive profits, which are kept within a relatively small group of large corporations.

An article in *Time Magazine* by journalism professor Victor Navasky, on the AOL-Time Warner merger in January 2000, pointed out:

> It has to do with what media critic Ben Bagdikan prophesied over a decade ago: that fewer and fewer corporations would come to dominate the media environment, resulting in the free-enterprise equivalent of a Ministry of Culture. It has to do with mega-communications conglomerates that are already bigger than the economies of countries whose monopolistic information policies we condemn as a violation of democratic values. It has to do, in other words, with the evil potential of bigness—what happens when the power to exercise total control over the information available to the American people passes from benign to the malign.

Although Navasky's "Ministry of Culture" scenario may have seemed extreme at the time, it manifested just over a year later, following the September 11 attacks. Whether consciously planned or not, all of America's major media corporations decided to support President George W. Bush, no matter what he did. Criticism of presidential policy all across the vastness of America virtually evaporated, and this consequently opened up a marked gap between the American perspective and the rest of the world including countries, which were (and continued to be) longtime allies and friends of the U.S.A. Americans felt misunderstood, but in fact it was probably the other way around. People all over the world watch American media coverage in addition to their own, but American media coverage of the rest of the world is scant in comparison. There has traditionally never been much demand for world news in America, which is not a good sign for a country that has become the world's *de facto* leader in an era that requires crucial and sensitive decision-making.

The debate over control and regulation of the media is not only about monopoly but also about content. The big media corporations of course argue against control in both areas, trumpeting the emotive "freedom" word, both of choice and speech. This predictably strikes a deep cord with the American populace but deserves a second look. How much is freedom of speech worth if it cannot be broadcast? Conversely, how much real choice do we have if we only hear a very narrow spectrum of views or are offered essentially the same products with only minor design and brand name variations? Within American politics and government over the last half decade, there have been many instances where lies, deception and inaccuracies have been successfully covered over simply by talking about something else . . . and of course, making sure it is broadcast widely. I do not deny that such tactics work in the short term but at what cost? The fact that it works so well should make us less secure not more because it is a weapon that can be used against us and more importantly, undermines our alleged core values.

Freedom of speech must certainly be prized and safeguarded, but on the other hand, we must realize that words and images, especially as they are being delivered today, have an extremely powerful effect. Just because they are not tangible does not mean they are not real.

Modern research is steadily confirming what Ageless Wisdom traditions have long upheld—that we are complex, multi-level beings who interact with our "external" environment all the time. Studies have found that even when we are in the womb (before our legal existence), we are affected by what our mothers ingest, feel, and experience. Modern medicine now accepts that stressful or polluted environments can be detrimental to health and it is beginning to admit the possibility that body, emotions, and mind are all interconnected. We can suffer the emotional and physical consequences of long past events of which we have no conscious memory.

Our actions can rarely be tracked to single chains of cause and effect (the current test of "reality), because they are the result of our cumulative, interactive experiences at many different levels of being and consciousness. In spite of our complexity, however, we tend at a basic level, like other species, to gravitate towards the more immediately pleasurable and recoil from the unpleasant or painful. Thus we tend to think short term rather than long. Moreover, the more a certain type of experience is repeated and the greater the intensity, identification, and participation we feel, the more we will be affected positively or negatively—it becomes an important part of our "reality."

The less balance, contentment, and stability we have internally, the more likely we are to look outside of ourselves for satisfaction and validation, and therefore the more likely we are to be swayed by outside influences. We instinctively know all this, and we even use this type of knowledge to train our pets—punishment for "bad" behavior and reward for "good." Yet, in spite of persuasive evidence to the contrary, we illogically deny that such strategies would succeed against ourselves. Even when we are proven to be predictable, we often justify it on the grounds that we are "freely" choosing to be predictable.

Just within the last fifty years, starting with the introduction of television, the average individual has been increasingly impacted by collective culture, morals, and attitudes delivered through the electronic media into the privacy of his or her home. As the delivery and content become more sophisticated, repetitive, coordinated, and concentrated, the impact of the various messages broadcast—i.e., the sense of reality and truth—becomes more convincingly "real." In other words, we are beginning to blur the boundaries between "virtual" reality and conventional reality.

With each new generation, the influence of the media increases because the exposure is earlier, more sophisticated, and more potent. The individual is affected not only directly by the media, but also indirectly by culture (the people around us), which itself has been shaped by the media. Thus, even if you do not have a TV or do not read the newspapers, their content and views will still impact on you through the people you meet (who do look at TV).

The TV has for some time been used as a baby sitter and has been reinforced by computers and video games, the most successful of which promote violence as entertainment. TV programs are being aimed at children as young as 2 years old, and as the child gets older, the barrage is reinforced by pre-teen and teen TV shows, movies, music videos, and magazines, many tied to the fashion industry. Fashion and movies have had a huge impact on body image and shape (among other things) and in turn has helped spawn the diet, exercise, and cosmetic surgery industries. Spin off TV shows and marketing add to the illusion that TV characters are real and in our virtual society, so they become! There is a hunger to know every trivial detail in the lives not only of the "stars," who come to be regarded almost as personal friends or family, but also of anyone currently in the media spotlight—"Fifteen Minute" celebrities.

As the child gets older, TV merchandising of fast-food toys and action figures glides seamlessly into high-priced sports shoes, designer clothes, high-tech items, and luxury cars, all of which in turn impact on the environment in which we live (right-hand quadrant). Many of these marketing campaigns are co-coordinated through psychologically sophisticated merchandising strategies, aimed at kids from an early age. Image (rather than substance), greed, power, materialism, sexual exploitation, and violence are used to sell goods and ideas to our children, and thus we should not be surprised when they come to ripeness in adulthood as just normal facets of life.

Children are particularly vulnerable targets because they are impressionable, malleable, and their developmental stages and tendencies are broadly predictable. A TV or computer screen in the home has become like a family friend or a substitute parent but with an intent that is not necessarily in the child's best interests—making a profit for a distant, uncaring corporation, providing a target for a pedophile etc. Children are an important marketing target group because they currently hold such sway with doting parents, guilty about their long hours away from home either at ultracompetitive jobs or indulging themselves as compensation for a stressful work environment. Activists, many psychologists themselves, are presently lobbying the American Psychological Association to discipline members who work as consultants and researchers for corporations targeting children.

As imagining and broadcasting technologies have become more sophisticated, entertainment has grown into a predominant and inescapable facet of modern culture. No longer confined to holidays and special social occasions, entertainment has become, for many people, a necessity for survival—a way of losing ourselves after a working day of stressful, mind-numbing work . . . rather like alcohol and drugs.

"Entertainment" is not restricted to TV, films, videos, music, and live performances but is now an essential ingredient in all aspects of our lives—advertising, news, business, religion, law, politics, etc. It is now common for news broadcasters and celebrities to give their personal views on current affairs, and these are often more influential than those of experts who have been studying or working for years within specific areas. This blurs the lines (even more) between the "real" and "unreal," fact and fiction. More often than not, you have to be a performer in order to be heard, irrespective of the merits of what you are saying. It is not surprising that most people on TV (especially in the U.S.A.) are good looking, especially the women. In many so-called "reality" shows, participants are specially selected and again turn out to be more-than-average attractive with personalities that are conductive to entertainment. The "reality" situation in which they are placed is unlike anything most people experience and is usually manipulated to elicit nudity or cruel behavior.

It is not a coincidence that American politics increasingly resembles TV. It is widely accepted that in public speaking, how you look and sound is more important than what you actually say. It is possible with good editing to make a powerful impact with brief images and sound bites. In the last fifty years, starting with John F. Kennedy, the most popular presidents have been photogenic and good TV performers. Ronald Reagan was a professional actor and has been followed into the political arena by Arnold Schwarzenegger, who recently became Governor of California with no political experience. His cynical but successful tactic was to limit any opportunity to answer questions and simply rely on his fame and continuous media exposure (which he got because of his already established fame.) He had no formal policies and many detractors but won easily. In 1998, professional wrestler, Jesse "The Body" Ventura, became the Governor of Minnesota, defeating one-time presidential candidate, Hubert Humphrey.

TV is steadily becoming a more obvious part of the political process in America. In the 2000 presidential election, CNN and other TV networks in many ways ran the election, selecting arbitrary panels of "experts" for ongoing commentary, hosting nationally broadcast presidential debates and even prematurely calling important voting results while ballots were still being cast in other parts of the country. Presidential candidates appeared on popular talk shows like *Oprah, Letterman, Jay Leno*, and *Larry King* in what were popularity contests rather serious interviews, due to limited time and the unspoken rule you cannot appear to be "negative" or even too intense. In these circumstances, being introspective, awkward before the cameras, or physically unattractive can (and often does) outweigh far more relevant and important qualities like experience, intelligence, honesty, integrity, and compassion. To rule the most powerful country in the world, you have to be cute! Although the media professionals initiate much of this manipulation, the public buys into it and therefore feeds it. As the Buddha pointed out long ago, all things are both conditioned and conditioning. Wilber might say the Four Quadrants of consciousness are interdependent and "interwoven."

The law enforcement and the justice systems have long provided entertainment fodder for TV, films, etc., and now television is using actual legal trials as "reality" entertainment. In America (and many other countries too), the O.J. Simpson trial, the impeachment of

President Clinton, the Clarence Thomas hearings, etc., have occupied weeks and months of prime-time TV and newspaper coverage.

The O.J. Simpson trial (like the Columbine School massacre which will be discussed later) was an unsettling microcosm of modern American life and included many of the elements we have been discussing in this book. Simpson was one of those rare individuals who had lived the American Dream to such an extent (until the murder of his wife and her companion) he could be a real, live, unembellished advertisement for it. He was a good-looking black kid from the "wrong side of the tracks" who became a national football hero and, after his playing days, got into the movies, living the high Hollywood lifestyle, replete with a mansion and a stunning blonde beauty for a wife. It was the kind of dream that built Hollywood and which no doubt still burns in many millions of hearts all over the world.

Like so many real-life Hollywood stories, there was a dark underside, and this one exploded in mythic fashion. The hero turned out to be a narcissistic womanizer and wife beater. Shortly after the wife, Nicole, separated from him and started living as a single woman, she and a male companion died in brutal, bloody circumstances, which soon pointed to her husband. About to be arrested, Simpson took off in his vehicle with a loaded gun, threatening suicide. He was followed for hours by dozens of police vehicles along the California highways, while fans held up signs of support by the roadside. The drama was televised live across America, interrupting regular programming. Simpson eventually surrendered, seemingly half-crazed.

It was decided that the trial be televised live, and this had a huge impact, since all participants would now be performing live before the cameras. It seemed that the script and trial strategy for the prosecution and judge would be one of the utmost postmodern, political correctness, and this would prove to be pivotal. The judge was neither black nor white but Japanese. The main prosecutors were a white woman (leading, of course) and a black man. Political correctness was also probably behind the strange decision to move the trial from the wealthy (mainly white) neighborhood where the crime was committed to downtown Los Angeles where the jury would be mostly black and less well off. They inexplicably agreed to exclude all mention of Simpson's nationally televised flight from evidence. All of this seemed to be (and in hindsight, was) what in racing or sporting terms would be called a massive handicap—a disadvantage accepted by a superior competitor in order to make the competition more equal.

During the trial, the defense team (much more famous and highly paid than the prosecution) stumbled upon unexpected treasure—evidence that one of the investigating police officers had made racist comments. The judge allowed this evidence into the trial even though much of Simpson's checkered past history was excluded. The lead defense lawyer, Johnnie Cochran, who was black, charismatic, and a talented preacher-actor-demagogue, saw his chance and took it. In stark contrast to his stiff, politically correct opposition, Cochran argued the unlikely but passion-stirring theory that Simpson was framed by racist white policemen, who were jealous of his rich lifestyle and beautiful white wife. The mostly black jury ignored a mountain of prosecution evidence and the highly improbable chances of such a complex, brilliant conspiracy. They found Simpson not guilty.

At the time of the trial, America was split into two distinct camps. Polls showed Blacks supporting O.J. Simpson, while Whites and other races (the majority) thought he was guilty. A few years after the trial, polls consistently revealed that a large majority of people of all races thought he was guilty. He was subsequently found responsible for the death of his wife and her friend, Ronald Goldman, in a civil suit brought by the victims' families and was ordered to pay damages, which remained largely unpaid since he claimed bankruptcy. Simpson presently lives in a large mansion in Florida, which allows bankrupts to keep their main residence.

Although this trial may not have a lasting or fundamental impact on America or the world, I have included it here because it contains many of the elements being discussed in this book and which define modern America. The trial riveted America, probably commanding more media attention (lasting months) than any other event since the assassination of President Kennedy. Some impressions of that trial which remain with me (in no particular order) include the inconsistency of evidence rules within the American legal system, the poor understanding of human nature on the part of many involved in the trial, the impotence and naivety of political correctness, the underestimation of the part that emotions play in our lives and of the power of racial identity, the significant influence of the media on the justice system, the ability of wealth to tilt the legal balance, the distorted priorities of the general public, and the monumental waste of resources and time in pursuit of "entertainment."

Complexity, Stress, and the Quick Fix

Complexity and stress may well be the most harmful yet least understood aspects of modern society and in particular of technology.

A fundamental and long-standing promise of consumer technology is that it will save you time and effort and provide greater convenience, thus allowing you opportunity for more important, meaningful, or pleasurable activities. Judging by the voracity with which we consume new technology, most people seem to wholeheartedly embrace this view of continuing progress and improvement through technology. Many even believe in the possibility of a technological paradise on earth—no work because of cheap energy and robotic labor; no pain because of miracle medical breakthroughs; happiness through virtual fantasies, etc.

Studies are beginning to show, however, that one of the characteristics of advancing technology is greater complexity and that few technological innovations touted as time saving, actually do. Indeed many people now complain of time shrinkage or deficit— the feeling there is not enough time to do all we think needs to be done. We constantly feel pressured and burdened even as we continue to buy new "tech" toys.

Complexity theories are sprouting, even though complexity itself is not new. Generally accepted characteristics of complex systems include a multiplicity of things, causal connections between components, interdependence of components, openness to the outside influences (since the system's boundaries are hard to define), synergy among components (the whole is greater than the sum of the individual parts), and nonlinear behavior, i.e., changes do not necessarily proceed evenly and predictably. Concerning the non-linear progression of events, Thomas Homer-Dixon noted in his book, *The Ingenuity Gap*:

> Perhaps the most striking evidence of how we can push the natural environment across a critical threshold was the hole in the stratospheric ozone layer that appeared over the Antarctic in the mid-1970s. At that time, scientific models assumed a roughly linear relationship between chlorofluorocarbon (CFC) emissions and stratospheric ozone depletion . . . as it turned out, if conditions are right, ozone destruction occurs at lightning speed.

Homer-Dixon feels that society is already too complex for us to handle and that an "ingenuity gap" has developed between our technical ingenuity and our lagging social ingenuity. Mentioning the work of complexity theorist Yaneer Bar-Yam, he writes:

> As modern human society becomes more complex than we are individually, it begins to exceed our adaptive ability. In effect we have too short a repertoire of responses to adjust effectively to our changing circumstances. As a result we try to simplify our social environment by limiting our exposure to it in various ways. In our everyday lives, for example, we retreat into tightly bounded sub-communities and in our work we specialize in narrow sub-professions.

In the passages above, Homer-Dixon is talking mainly about complexity in systems (Wilber's lower right quadrant), but if his observations are accurate, we would expect to see similarities and interconnections within other quadrants.

I believe that what we call "stress" is the impact of complexity on the individual (upper left quadrant). Dr. Hans Selye, who originated the theory of a "stress syndrome," describes it as a non-specific adaptation disease that can give rise to a variety of symptoms. It is "non-specific" in the sense that the patient's condition cannot be linked to a single cause but is likely the result of many, probably interdependent causes. It is an "adaptation" disease because the disease itself is caused by our (inadequate) response to change. Crudely speaking, we are comparatively rigid and conditioned (by our environment, attitudes, belief systems, etc.) in our reactions and thus tend to over or under-react to situations, often relying on our basic hereditary response of "fight or flight." In Homer-Dixon's passage above, "limiting our exposure" and retreating into sub-communities or sub-professions would be examples of what is regarded as "flight" in stress terminology.

Stress not only triggers emotional feelings within us but an accompanying variety of biochemical and physical reactions (upper right quadrant) as well. The interconnection of mind, emotions, and physical body, long a basic principle of Eastern medicine, is now finally being acknowledged in the West.

Dr. Hans Selye identified three basic phases in the stress syndrome. The first stage is the "alarm" or fight or flight stage, when we first encounter the stressors. The second stage is called the "resistance" phase, wherein the mind-body system tries to accommodate itself to the stressors. This resistance stage consumes a lot of basic "adaptation energy," and over time, drains and weakens the overall system. The third and final stage is that of "exhaustion"— sudden and widespread collapse.

The second stage seems to me to correspond to the stage of denial. It is common for people to be aware that they face (perhaps severe) health risks, yet they do not make lifestyle changes because they feel they will be the lucky exceptions to the rule. They assert, "There may or may not be a problem, but I'll tough it out and get through it. It hasn't defeated me so far, so I will keep on doing it my way. My luck is bound to change." For example, most individuals know that smoking, drinking, bad eating habits, and chronic stress are not healthy, but few try seriously to change unless they get some kind of shock. Often, even that is not enough to bring about permanent change. Not surprisingly, this same pattern of reaction is common in our approach to communal and global problems—put it off and maybe it will change by itself or our children will find some miracle solution.

The third "exhaustion" stage of the stress syndrome is usually severe and traumatic. It often does result in life changes, but not always. For others, by the time this stage manifests, it is already too late. Although stress-related diseases are vague and non-specific, they are "real" enough to be filling our hospitals and mortuaries.

There are similar signs of complexity and stress within our collective lives and living environment. This should not be surprising since, as we have seen, all quadrants/aspects of our lives are connected and interdependent. We do not have one big problem but many interrelated ones. The planet itself is under severe stress—accumulating pollution and toxins in air, water, and soil, the hole in the ozone layer, global warming, impending resource and water shortages (of potable and irrigation water), and climatic volatility, which has already resulted in unusually high levels of death and destruction. Fish stocks are declining rapidly, species of flora and fauna are becoming extinct at an unprecedented, and new "super" viruses and insects are appearing in response to drugs and pesticides. Cross-species infections like mad cow disease, AIDS, and West Nile virus are increasing and will probably continue to do so with more widespread genetic engineering. The health of the planet and human health are interrelated because we literally eat, drink, and breathe the planet.

In 1992, at the Earth Summit in Rio, a document entitled, *World Scientists' Warning to Humanity* was released. It began:

> Human beings and the natural world are on a collision
> course. Human activities inflict harsh and often irreversible
> damage on the environment and on critical resources. If not
> checked, many of our current practices put at serious risk
> the future that we wish for human society and the plant

and animal kingdoms and may so alter the living world that
it will be unable to sustain life in the manner that we know.
Fundamental changes are urgent if we are to avoid the
collision our present course will bring about . . . . No more
than one or a few decades remain before the chance to avert
the threats we now confront will be lost.

Human activities affect not only the planet but also other
human beings. As mentioned before, there is an increasing gap
between the rich and poor; population is increasing rapidly in the
poorer countries; more people are dying as a result of pollution
and stress; disaffected groups and even individuals have access to
increasingly potent weapons like computers, viruses, gases, and
black market nuclear weapons material. The Y2K scare and the
"hacker" attacks on government and business computer systems
are a warning about our over dependence on computer systems.
The twenty-first-century technologies of robotics, genetics, and
nanotechnology will greatly add to the scale of both unforeseen
error and deliberate sabotage. In addition, they will create far more
complexity, since they will change the very concept of what it
means to be human.

After an initial stage of collective "alarm" about the
environment, computers, terrorism, and energy shortage, we seemed
to have settled into a "resistance" stage of accommodating ourselves
to our new situation. Since Reagan, Thatcher, and the fall of the
Soviet Union, the Western world has become infatuated with the
Free Market. The "economy" is now our highest priority (even over
terrorism) while other issues have been neglected—the
environment, energy, social services, education, health, etc. The
radical implications of the approaching technologies are barely
discussed apart from the dramatic issue of cloning. As with
individuals, the thinking is, "We're ahead so far—don't mess with
a winning strategy." As regards this attitude, there are two
considerations worth pondering: Firstly, not everyone is winning.
The vast majority of the planet's population is "losing." Secondly,
if or when the bad news comes, it may come in the form of

devastating collapses or blows, rather than a gradual deterioration—in other words, the "exhaustion" stage of the stress syndrome or the rapid "non-linear" progression recognized in complexity theory.

In accordance with our scientism conditioning, we seem to be waiting for the quick fix . . . the magic pill that will cure all ills. Most people seem to be investing their hope in technology. Others are waiting for a miraculous religious revival or the dawning of a new spiritual age that will transform our consciousness as never before.

I do not think the answer is to abandon all technological innovation but to better understand both technology and ourselves so that we can make wiser choices regarding technology. Not everything that is technologically possible is appropriate, since everything has a cost. Lusting after every new technological toy amounts to an addiction, which is not conducive to balanced decision making.

We urgently need more (spiritual) evolution in the left-hand quadrants or in Homer-Dixon's terms, we need more "social ingenuity." In short, there is an imbalance or gap between the complexity engendered by our (right hand) technological evolution and our present ability to handle it. It is of the utmost importance that we turn our attention to the possibilities of human evolution and advancement, as have been described in so many different Ageless Wisdom spiritual traditions from all parts of the world.

If we have no sense of self or purpose beyond our mundane duties, roles, and distractions, then we are left with just increasing fragmentation, conflict, and complexity, which beyond a certain level, will become overwhelming. The more information we generate, the more there is to process. The more we seek to control, the more responsibility and decision making we automatically undertake, thereby increasing the probability of error.

When it gets to be too much for our psyches to handle ("fight" strategy does not work), then we turn to "flight"—shutting down, temporarily losing ourselves in the minutiae of our lives, in simplistic hope and idealization or in alcohol, drugs, sex, etc. Those who can afford it, travel all over the world trying to "get away from it all," not realizing that "it" is inside themselves. In the process, they destroy those rare sanctuaries not already overrun with humanity.

I believe that this overwhelming stress and complexity is a major factor in our general silence and inaction even though we realize that there is something radically wrong with our present approach to life. We do not know what the answer is, and we are troubled, but we do not have the time and energy to inquire, much less fight, so we put ourselves to sleep. Often we use more technology to help us in our temporary escape, and in so doing, we enmesh ourselves even further in complexity.

The modern sage J.D. Krishnamurti advised that complexity cannot be overcome by more complexity but only by simplicity. The simplest thing that we can do is to take stock of ourselves here and now and ask ourselves not "What do I want?" but "What do I need to do? What response to life is appropriate?" What you want and what is apt may be one and the same thing, but it is not always that way. If we all begin to respond appropriately moment by moment, then complexity will rapidly fall away.

Alienation, Dependence, and Virtual Reality

Because the scientific mindset is one of abstraction and analysis, it often leads not only to fragmentation and complexity but also alienation and amorality—a sense of being cut off, adrift, numb, feeling that nothing matters or makes any sense. Although this may seem absurd if we think of one person analyzing one problem, it should be remembered that our whole lives are lived in this manner, and our social and cultural systems also reflect these dynamics.

In analysis, when we observe, we distance ourselves from the object of observation or study, which is then intellectually isolated and assigned to theoretical boxes. As we study each box more closely, we discover sub-compartments, which in turn become new boxes. More detailed knowledge of each box and sub-compartment allows us greater control and manipulation, for which we are generally rewarded by society. In this manner new fields of study, specialties and government departments proliferate.

After a while, however, we find ourselves increasingly pressured and alienated from life as we struggle to control the proliferating concerns, responsibilities, and roles in our daily lives. There are so many details to monitor "out there" we gradually lose sight of any underlying, coherent purpose; we have no time to inquire even if we want to. We are all hustling to play the "game" better than the next person because this means more immediate rewards, but few know what the real purpose of the game is or the long-term consequences. In the process, we lose a sense of morality and value, in the most profound sense. There is nothing but the next dollar or next cheap thrill—mere quantity, which yields diminishing returns of satisfaction.

We can clearly see this process in big organizations—corporations, universities, governments, the army, the police, etc. In order to climb the ladder of your particular organization, you are expected to play according to its "rules," not only within the working day, but also often after hours and in your social life. There is subtle but tremendous pressure to "fit in" and be a "team player" or else you might be kicked off the team. As an auditor and accountant, I have witnessed this in every single business I have encountered—literally hundreds—from the factory floor to the boardroom.

In time, constant high-pressure work may become an addiction, which is justified in terms of prosperity. Matters and relations outside of work are neglected as well as the worker's health. Time away from work may be spent manically "blowing off steam" with alcohol, drugs, or sex. The worker loses perspective and is dominated by internal corporate priorities and values. Unfortunately, what is good for the organization is not necessarily what is good for its individual workers or for society at large. The organizational criminals that come to public attention from time to time represent only the tip of the proverbial iceberg and should elicit neither surprise nor shock. What is surprising is that we are still surprised by this kind of behavior. Ruthlessness, corruption and manipulation are part of acceptable business and political practice, so long as it is kept within socially acceptable bounds or preferably, out of sight.

It is becoming common in daily life to encounter representatives of corporations and institutions who mechanically recite their particular institution's rules or policies as sufficient justification for their action, even if these are illogical, unfair, or just barely legal. This machinelike interaction is not a coincidence since many of them are reading from monitored scripts and have no authority to make decisions—thereby paving the way for real machines to take over. Sometimes, in frustration, I challenge them, as fellow human beings, to step out of their corporate mindset and contemplate the logic or morality of what they are doing and consider the long-term implications for the quality of human life— depersonalization, lack of real choice, steady replacement of humans by computers even as humans are pitted against each other for dwindling jobs. In most cases, all I get is yet another repetition of the rules, as if I am somehow talking a foreign language. Occasionally, however, I have encountered off-the-record agreement even at the managerial level. Some even reveal to me how such dynamics operate in their own company.

These alienation processes are not confined to large organizations. If we sincerely look within ourselves, we will find them operating. The sense of a whole, coherent self is rapidly giving way to a multitude of boxes/roles/personae, often with no apparent connection and sometimes even in conflict with each other—child, parent, worker, family person, lover, spouse, friend, artist, athlete, savior/saved, etc. It is becoming common to hear people talking as if they were separate from their bodies. We now replace body parts as casually as we change car engine parts including genitals, breasts and faces. In a similar manner, we feel alienated from spouses, children, parents, local communities, nature, etc. Internet friends are often prized over the flesh-and-blood kind, because we have become accustomed to the computer-generated sense of separation and power, which we can control by simply turning "off" or "on."

Constantly playing all these different roles, we begin to feel fragmented, alienated, confused, and overwhelmed. The opportunity to pursue many different activities and personae may be exhilarating at first, but over time it wears us out, and we then lose the sense of who we really are or what is the purpose of life. Moreover, for many of us, under all this frenetic activity, a nagging sense of emptiness and purposelessness lurks.

Only a few generations ago, most people lived in the countryside, engaged in agriculture, physically working the land and tending animals. Today half the world lives in congested, noisy, polluted cities, a growing number of which exceed the 10 million mark. This represents a tremendous change in lifestyle within a comparatively short period of time. David Suzuki, geneticist and host of the TV series, *The Nature of Things*, writes in his book, *The Sacred Balance*, about the resulting alienation and artificiality:

> The most destructive aspect of cities is the profound schism created between human beings and nature. In a human-made environment, surrounded by animals and plants of our choice, we feel ourselves to have escaped the limits of nature. Weather and climate impinge on our lives with far less immediacy. Food is often highly processed and comes in packages, revealing little of its origins in the soil or telltale blemishes, blood, feathers or scales. We forget the source of our water and energy, the destiny of our garbage and sewage . . . Cut off from the sources of our food and the consequences of our way of life, we imagine a world under our control and will risk or sacrifice almost anything to make sure our way of life continues.

The advent of the personal screen—TV, computer, video games, mobile communication devices, etc.—has greatly reinforced the illusory notion of reality as a personal, insulated bubble that we can control. We can scan the Internet and literally hundreds of TV channels. The media encourages the fantasy that we somehow have a personal relationship and connection with the media superstars that are paraded before us. Many people have "virtual" sex and relationships on the Internet and look forward to increasing sophistication and advances in the field of virtual reality because the notion of having complete control of your personal fantasy is so very seductive—you do not have to deal with real people.

Ironically, although the concept of virtual reality may seem very modern and exciting to many people, the Buddha pointed out over 2,500 years ago that we are the result of what we think . . . that the mind creates its own sense of reality. He also pointed out that our suffering arises within, and therefore it is only within ourselves that we can find release from suffering—by letting go. Countless generations of people before the Buddha and after him have been trying to beat suffering, latterly with technology, but all have failed. The reasons for this will be discussed in chapters three and four.

The cost of each of us retreating into our own mental fantasy bubble is that we become increasingly cut off from the totality and higher potential of ourselves, from real relationships with other people and from our environment. We then tend to make inconsistent and narrow-minded decisions, many of which are determined by the compulsion to maintain our fantasies.

In our present "high," we imagine we can control the whole world. In reality, our illusion of control is very delicate and precarious. It depends on the continuance of a very complex and fragile infrastructure that can be manipulated, attacked, or broken down through error or oversight. In the summer of 2003, fifty million people in the eastern part of North America lost power because a tree fell on some power lines! Those who live in large cities know what happens when routines are disrupted for any significant length of time, whether by power breakdowns, extreme weather, industrial strikes or shortages. "Normal" people quickly become desperate and aggressive, abandoning social niceties and conventions in order to get their perceived share or rights. Law and order may rapidly break down into looting, rioting, raping, etc.

Imagine what would happen in more extreme circumstances like an attack by another country, a limited terrorist attack featuring germ or nuclear warfare or even a computer attack that targets our essential operating systems? The Y2K scare at the beginning of the year 2000 and the subsequent "hacker" attacks should be a warning that such events are not only possible but probable. We are so dependent on computers now that a single cyber-terrorist can wreak havoc. Genetics have now enabled germ warfare experts to target specific genetic groups. Some futurists predict that in the not-too-distant future (before 2020), we will be fighting each other over plain old water—humble, but essential. We can live without oil and computers but not water.

From both individual and collective standpoints we need to make sense of our world and find purpose and value, because crucial decisions are at hand. For this, we have to be in touch with our world and not cut ourselves off from it. If we completely open ourselves to "ordinary life" rather than trying to escape from it, we will find treasures and gifts beyond our expectations.

Sex, Violence, and the Sensational

If we examine the content of popular media and entertainment, which both shape and reflect popular culture, certain items jump out at us—sex, violence, sensationalism, and celebrity. The latter includes not only interest in the lives of media personalities, film and music stars, etc., but also people who temporarily excite popular interest—usually because of sex, violence, or sensationalism. The 1960s media artist Andy Warhol predicted everyone would be famous for fifteen minutes, and that prediction is now being used by an increasing number of people as a reason to get their Warholian "Fifteen Minutes of Fame" at whatever costs that may entail, sometimes including murder. Warhol was no doubt insightful, but his utterance also had its own self-fulfilling effect, as we should expect from the interaction of the four "interwoven" quadrants of reality.

As usual, there are two simplistic and opposite ways of interpreting these cultural trends. On one hand, many within the popular, traditional religions see society degenerating into godlessness, sin, and decadence, which the *Concise Oxford Dictionary* defines as, "a state of moral or cultural deterioration; self-indulgent." There is *prima facie* evidence to support such a contention, especially as regards godlessness, cultural deterioration, and self-indulgence.

The opposite way of perceiving these developments is as an expression of freedom, liberation, and sophistication. According to this view, the religions in the past imposed arbitrary, self-serving, onerous (often male-dominated) moral rules on society, but now we have outgrown them because we are more mature, scientific, worldly-wise and our technology allows us greater potential. A motley crew sails under this banner—the entertainment and media industries, entrepreneurs in general, civil libertarians, some feminists, intellectuals and artists, hedonists, followers of scientism, performers, etc. This perspective seems to be winning the war of public opinion so far, but the fundamentalists are still a strong and volatile force.

Although society still tends to look at issues in terms of just two opposite, contrasting views (the stuff of TV debates and radio talk shows), life is of course far more complex. In this regard, I often think of the old story of a group of blind men experiencing an elephant for the first time. Each of them passionately and accurately describes the part of the elephant he is touching—tusk, tail, flank, leg, etc. (Yes, even Nazis have some rationale for their attitudes.) Yet even though each of them is convinced about what is "real" based on his own experience, none of them describes other parts, much less the whole elephant.

Some of the greatest Ageless Wisdom spiritual teachers have pointed out that true freedom is not merely doing whatever you feel like doing, but freeing yourself from your compulsive and limiting patterns of behavior. Thus although having numberless sexual partners may appear like freedom, if sex is a compulsive addiction, then that person is not truly free and his or her behavior may in addition entail serious health and social consequences. If you do not go beyond your patterns, you are limited in the scope of your response and forced to repeat your behavioral patterns albeit in slightly different guises.

Our preoccupation with sex, violence, and sensationalism should not be surprising given our foregoing discussions. In spite of our amazing scientific and technological advances and unprecedented prosperity, life for many people feels empty and meaningless and at the same time, increasingly confusing, changeable, and stressful.

Sex and violence are obvious, accessible, and immediate ways to make us feel real, alive, special, and meaningful—even if only for a fleeting moment. Because other people share this fascination, we can also use sex and violence to draw attention to ourselves so that we can stand out in an increasingly anonymous world. "Look at me naked! I exist!" This dynamic seems similar to that of the schizophrenic who inflicts serious injuries on himself in order to ground/center himself in the physical and thus temporarily escape the confusion and disorientation of his own multiple mind-generated "realities."

In considering these matters, it must be remembered that these dynamics involve all four Wilberian quadrants of consciousness. This behavior is not only a reaction by individuals to the barrenness of modern technology-driven society, but it is a (highly profitable) product, created and marketed by many segments of society. As Herbert Marcuse accurately pointed out back in the 1960s, capitalism has learned to overcome its opponents not only through military might but also by integrating them into its "system." Thus the U.S.A. is no longer (so far) attacking their old Communist enemies with missiles and armies but with trade and the export of American culture. Within individual countries, underground, anti-establishment, "outrageous," counterculture activities and movements all gradually become assimilated into the mainstream profit-making machine. The sex and rock and roll of the 1960s youth counterculture have subsequently made billions of dollars for mainstream industries.

A current and apposite example of this process is the

phenomenally successful merchandising of American black ghetto "gangsta" rap music and lifestyle to young people not only in the U.S.A. but also worldwide—Europe, Africa, Russia, Philippines, Japan, etc. Interestingly enough, it includes all the elements under discussion—sex, violence, and celebrity. Common themes for the music and accompanying videos are pimps, whores, gangsters, and "playas" (predatory males and females using sex and power in whatever form to attain their goals, whether sexual conquest or material and/or monetary profit). Often the heroes of these pieces get even with those who look down on them by attaining fame and fortune, which they then flaunt.

The fact that all of this is broadcast and sold worldwide means that it has been embraced by the big media corporations who market the music CDs, videos, magazines, films, TV reviews, games, clothes and more. Why is this so attractive and successful? There is sensuality and sexuality—voluptuous women and Adonis-like men gyrating and caressing themselves (and others) in near nudity. Sometimes we also get violent lyrics and/or video clips. All of this is sold (by the big corporations) as young, vibrant, freshly creative, anti-establishment, "cool" and in some contorted way, politically correct, since much of it features Blacks, women, gays, or "teen rebels" justifiably venting their rage and claiming their power!

This current marketing phenomenon is of course the ever-present, time-tested American Dream dressed up in modern urban garb. The seemingly insignificant person of humble origins overcomes overwhelming odds and "makes it," just like the big movie and rock stars! Like the lottery (also popular), a very few win through, and they are ostentatiously paraded in order to "prove" the validity of the system and thus continue to fuel it. The vast majority, however, have their lottery dreams crumble to dust. Social improvements are neglected and the gap between the rich and poor widens.

Even the exploitation of the Black rap culture, however, pales in comparison with the omnipresent marketing of female sexuality and in particular the female body. Ironically, women are prominent in this endeavor. Most fashion editors who continue to favor unnaturally slender (sometimes emaciated) women models are themselves women; women's magazines are increasingly featuring articles on cosmetic surgery (although carefully stopping short of outright recommendation). Some feminists have contended that the phenomenon of women selling themselves as sexual objects and doing whatever they wish to enhance their bodies represents an evolutionary step forward since this is a form of "power". Women engaged in manipulation and exploitation is somehow seen as superior to men doing the same.

It is ironic that one of the main complaints of the 1960s liberation movements was that we placed too much emphasis on physical differences and appearances—whether gender, sexuality, color, etc. Now, thanks largely to the reaction of the1980s, the body culture is predominant, leading to unrealistic and extreme body shapes, from the rail thin but full-breasted model to the exaggerated (grotesque) bodybuilder physiques for women as well as men. This has created numerous sub-industries including weight-loss and bodybuilding drugs, cosmetic surgery, eating disorder and addiction treatment centers. It seems that even as we try to make our bodies more beautiful, we become more dissatisfied with them because we see more "imperfections" and improvement possibilities. We have rapidly extended our throwaway culture to include human beings—not beautiful, entertaining, young, enough, etc. We seem to ignore the fact that the more we all embrace this attitude, the more dispensable and worthless we individually become. Our "shelf life" ever shortens.

Although the sexualizing of our culture is more damaging than we seem to think, the unholy alliance of technology and violence is far more sinister and dangerous. Technology has not only enormously increased the killing capacity of weapons but also has progressively encouraged us to dissociate ourselves from the effects of our violence. Moreover, violence has been increasingly and successfully promoted, especially by Hollywood, as an acceptable form of entertainment.

The invention of the gun and cannon introduced a much more

detached and devastating form of killing than had ever existed in human history. It is far easier to shoot someone from a distance than to go toe-to-toe with him or her with sharp metal, wood, or stone. Dynamite and machine guns increased both the devastation and killing distance, as did tanks, planes, and missiles. The slaughter in World War I trenches became the aerial carpet-bombing and atomic bombs of World War II, which slaughtered hundreds of thousands from high above. These were the first great WMDs (Weapons of Mass Destruction). Now we can kill across the globe via symbols on a screen, exactly as in a video game. People's bodies and homes are still shattered, but we do not have to see it. It thus makes it easier for us to kill and ignore the consequences of our killing. We have been exposed to the personal history of each September 11 victim, yet we cannot even get an approximate idea of the numbers (surely many thousands) of those killed in "collateral damage" in our "liberation" of Afghanistan and Iraq.

Other subjective factors connected with technology are also operating, for example, curiosity, ego, and wanting to play God. The U.S. military could have aborted work on the atomic bomb after Germany surrendered in 1945. They continued, largely because they and their scientists were curious! They wanted to see how a real bomb would actually work, even though they were aware of the dangers of nuclear fallout as well as the likelihood of an ensuing nuclear arms race. In spite of these grave dangers, they proceeded to drop not one bomb but two—on Hiroshima and Nagasaki, destroying the cities and killing hundreds of thousands, mostly innocent civilians. Not even one bomb was necessary since the war was effectively over. To compound the folly, efforts after the war to control the development of nuclear weapons failed because of fear and hate on all sides, and within four years (1949), the Soviets exploded their first bomb. The thrill of U.S. superiority was short lived, and the cold war ensued for forty years, almost exploding into an all-out nuclear war during the Cuban Missile Crisis. President George W. Bush is once again attempting to give the U.S.A. missile "superiority."

Even if no further nuclear wars or major terrorist atrocities occur, it is a crime against humanity to pour such vast resources into arsenals (nuclear and other), which in the best-case scenario, we destroy as obsolete. How much medicine, food, health care, housing, and pure drinking water can we get for a single fighter plane or a barrage of cruise missiles, costing over $1 million each? Many would scoff that it is naïve to think in those terms. It is only naïve if we think it is. If we put as much effort and resources into peace as we do into war, we would have peace by now. Rather than seriously try to find peace and harmony within and among ourselves, we have laboriously and at great cost developed the capability to destroy civilization as we know it in order to restrain ourselves—a strategy appropriately called MAD (mutually assured destruction). Peace is indeed a difficult process, but the average person seems unaware of the fact that there are powerful forces, which have a vested interest in fighting and in wars. Many in public life openly declare that war is the best way to stimulate the economy!

As the power of our technology increases, the potential for error or conscious destruction increases. Bill Joy, information technology and web pioneer, has become very alarmed at the possibilities of the future, especially after meeting with several pioneers of the new technologies. He cautions:

> The 21st century technologies—genetics, nanotechnology and robotics—are so powerful that they can spawn whole new classes of accidents and abuses. Most dangerously, for the first time, these accidents and abuses are widely within the range of individuals or small groups. They will not require large facilities or rare raw materials. Knowledge alone will enable the use of them.

We have not only increased the power of our weapons but have continually exposed ourselves and our children to images of violence and through virtual reality games, teach them how to efficiently kill in realistic situations. In his book, *High Tech, High Touch*, futurist John Naisbitt described how the U.S. military and the video games industry worked together to produce killing video

games that could be used both for military training and for
commercial sale, i.e., for marketing violence as a form of
entertainment to children. He observed:

> The number-one entertainment in America today is media
> and the number-one genre of content is violence. Yet we do
> not take it seriously . . . . It is a radical idea to suggest that
> screens and their content are real. But the consequences of
> thinking of them as fantasy, as virtual, as benign are
> devastating.

Retired Lt. Col. David Grossman, author of *The Psychological
Cost of Learning to Kill in War and Society*, warns:

> Video games hardwire young people for shooting at humans.
> The entertainment industry conditions the young in exactly
> the same way the military does.

This training is not only in marksmanship, but also in cutting
off from caring and the bloody consequences of killing. It has proven
successful not only during the Gulf War, where many kills from
airplanes or tanks were mere disappearing blips on a screen, but in
several school shootings. In the latter, teenagers, who had been training
with video games for hundreds of hours, shot with much more deadly
accuracy than the average full-time policeman or soldier.

Because adults do not play video games as much as children, they
tend to underestimate both their scope and their impact. In the U.S.,
the electronic games industry's sales figures are more than twice those
of movies. Many of video games' covers are deliberately cartoon like to
create the illusion, especially for parents, that the product is childish
and harmless. Stephen Kline, director of the Media Analysis Lab at
Simon Fraser University, concludes from his research:

> Being a spectator in violence is less engaging than interacting
> with violence in interactive media. We've found it to be more
> emotionally dynamic in terms of blood flow and stress levels.

The 1999 Columbine High School massacre in Littleton, Colorado, is worthy of consideration because it includes many of the dangerous and volatile dynamics we have been discussing, and because it has been the inspiration for subsequent mass killings in schools. Two boys, aged seventeen and eighteen, from affluent white families walked into their school, dressed in black leather trench coats and armed with shot guns, and methodically proceeded to kill fourteen fellow students and a teacher. They then killed themselves. Twenty-eight more people were injured and thirty pipe bombs, which failed to explode, were found scattered around the school. A video recorded by the boys prior to the slaughter revealed that they planned in detail how they could kill 250 people at the school!

Subsequent investigations revealed a not-uncommon case of teenage angst, wherein the boys felt themselves treated as social outcasts and wanted to take revenge on their enemies—get even, "show them." Not so long ago, this might have exploded into a knife or baseball bat attack with far less serious consequences. There are several elements to their story, however, which are peculiar to modern-day America and which still exist now.

Perhaps even stronger than their desire for revenge was a lust for recognition, for being acknowledged as somebody, anybody— a dark "Fifteen Minutes of Fame." The massacre was planned and scripted for over a year, drawing for ideas on films like *Natural Born Killers* and *The Basketball Diaries*, and video games, especially the popular combat-killing game, *Doom*, which they spent many solitary hours playing. On their video, the boys boasted that this would be the best-ever school massacre, that it would be like something out of *Doom* and that famous movie directors like Steven Spielberg and Quentin Tarantino (maker of the explicitly violent *Reservoir Dogs* and *Pulp Fiction*) would be fighting over their story. They talked about how, in memories and nightmares, they would live forever, haunting especially the survivors of their planned massacre. Their parents seemed to be well off and caring though somewhat preoccupied with their own jobs and middle-class lives. They did not inquire into what the boys were doing with their time, even after several warning signals.

It was found that the Columbine killers spent a lot of time on the Internet, from which they got their bomb-making information. One of the killers had a personal website in which he listed the types of pipe bombs he possessed and described how and why he was about to embark on a killing spree. On the website, he also threatened a fellow student, whose parents alerted the police. The police checked out the website but did nothing (even though the killers had recently been caught breaking into a van) because they were too busy with other "more important" crimes. They did not even bother to notify the boys' parents. In their video, the killers revealed they were aware that no one took them seriously, and this made them all the more determined to make their mark. The final (or perhaps primary) factor in the enabling of this massacre was the ease with which the teenagers could obtain weapons and ammunition. The bullets were bought over the counter at K-Mart.

Much of popular culture is based on trying to make us feel more alive—through sex, drugs, violence, entertainment, thrills, the "Fifteen Minutes of Fame", etc. Mark Chapman said his primary motive for killing ex-Beatle John Lennon in1980 was to "steal his fame," and since he is still, after more than 20 years, being interviewed about his crime, he has succeeded. This kind of desperation suggests that in spite of all our high-tech activity, bravado, and seeming control, we still feel deadened, impoverished, unfulfilled, and meaningless inside. Ever more technology or artificial thrill seeking is not going to fill this internal void but will likely make our lives even more complex, stressful, and alienated.

The Antidote: Simplicity and Inner Direction

Modern society drives us to ever faster and more complex activity. The "carrot" incentive is greater consumer power, whether you exercise it to acquire material goods, "trophy" spouses and houses, leisure activity or notoriety. The "stick" disincentive is that if you do not do the job required of you, which increasingly involves mastery of new technology and longer working hours, then there are many others willing to take your place. We are subject to a time-tested formula of greed, ambition, competition, and fear made all the more effective and widespread by technology and elusive, anonymous market forces. There is no longer a particular tyrant or crooked boss at whom we can point our finger and run out of town. We are victims of the elusive "system," which we ourselves create and maintain.

As complexity increases, we tend to lose sight of cause and effect and thus underestimate or not count the real costs of our actions. This is true not only of the effects of our actions on others but also on ourselves. On the personal level, "stress" (which includes a wide range of mind-body factors and disorders) is taking a far higher toll on our mental, emotional, and physical health than is popularly acknowledged. In the true spirit of "scientism," we think it is not "real" because it is not something physically or immediately obvious like a wound, food poisoning, or weight gain. New psychological and other disorders, however, are appearing all the time. One of the latest is "information fatigue syndrome" with symptoms that include depression, anxiety, insomnia, inability to focus, high blood pressure, and social withdrawal. John Seely Brown writes in his book, *The Social Life of Information*:

> On an average weekday, a major newspaper contains more information than any contemporary of Shakespeare's would have acquired in a lifetime . . . There's no way human sensory evolution has caught up with that kind of deluge.

Worn down by non-stop activity, deadlines, competition, social change, and complexity, we tend to become disoriented, alienated, withdrawn, and frustrated, at times murderously so. Life for many is a soulless grind with little redeeming virtue or meaning. Our attempts at escapism do not take away our problems but often create more—alcoholism, drug use, sex addiction, obesity, domestic violence, suicide, broken homes, etc. Stress-related diseases may be non-specific, hard to define, and thus seemingly "not really real," but they nevertheless are a major and serious health threat in the developed Western countries, filling hospital beds, mental wards, and cemetery plots.

The costs of this lifestyle are also collective, impacting on those around us and on our environment. Unlike much of humanity's past, many of us are competing with each other not for food and survival but for conspicuous consumption. We are devouring not square miles or even hundreds of square miles, but the planet itself. In the "global village", the number of big winners in this consumption game is minimal in comparison to the losers, many of whom are literally living on and off of garbage dumps in Third World monster cities. Some scientists are already making detailed plans for a selected few to leave the planet because we are wasting it at such an accelerated rate.

We have made the fundamental mistake of thinking that technology can take away human suffering, not realizing that our suffering largely arises within, since it is the result of human thoughts, emotions, and actions. Even though most people in the West have experienced an astronomic rise in their standards of living, there are widespread signs of dissatisfaction. Will just a few more material goods and tech toys make us content? Technology is not only unlikely to bring us fulfillment, but it may pose a threat to our very existence through error, war, or losing the evolutionary battle with our own technology. The point has been made that in a Free Market society, if intelligent robots are more efficient and powerful than humans, then they should control the planet's resources.

What can we do? One of the simplest, cheapest, and most immediate actions we can take is to set aside time to do nothing . . . apart from paying "bare attention" to what is taking place within us. If we do this skillfully (which is not the same as daydreaming or having an internal dialogue), we will experience astonishing results. We may call this practice a particular form of "meditation," or we may think of it as developing the internal knowledge, skill, and ingenuity to help us to understand, balance, and better utilize our scientific and technological prowess in the "external" world.

On the measurable, physical plane, meditation has been proven to help with a variety of medical problems. Dr. Dean Ornish included meditation as one of the life habits his patients undertook in order to successfully reverse the effects of serious heart disease. Dr. Jon Kabat-Zinn used Buddhist mindfulness meditation to reduce stress, cultivate relaxation, and relieve pain. When asked by TV journalist Bill Moyers, "If it would have been as successful if you'd called it 'Courses in Meditation' instead of 'Stress-Reduction Clinic,'" Kabat-Zinn replied:

> I can guarantee you that it wouldn't have been. Who would have wanted to go to a meditation class? But when people walk down the halls in this hospital and they see signs saying, "Stress Reduction and Relaxation," they respond, "I could use that . . ." One way to look at meditation is as a kind of intrapsychic technology that's been developed over a couple of thousand years by traditions that know a lot about the mind/body connection.

Although meditation can bring surprising health benefits (which will be discussed later), it is of course ideally suited to problems of the emotions, mind, and spirit. The more we dispassionately watch ourselves, the more the jumble of ideas, beliefs, goals, desires, and "truths," which seem so compelling and real in our frenetic everyday state of consciousness, will fade, and a new awareness and understanding arise in their place. We will begin to see life in terms of that Ageless Wisdom teachers have long taught and modern physicists like Bohm are beginning to describe: "An inseparable quantum interconnectedness of the whole universe is the fundamental reality."

When our actions emanate from direct seeing of "what is," rather than from fixed ideas and beliefs that we have inherited or adopted, our whole life will be transformed. We will spontaneously respond to life one moment at a time. What to do and what is right and wrong will be "obvious," but in a way that is very different from those whose sense of the "obvious" is derived from belief systems, whether religious, political, or otherwise. The former tends to be more inclusive, flexible, compassionate, and aware of the interdependence of all life. The latter tends towards rigidity and the division of life into right and wrong, good and bad, saved and damned etc.

Such a shift in the source of our action would address many of the problems we have been discussing. Complexity and stress will immediately begin to dissolve. The quality of our lives will improve because we will be able to recognize quality rather than trying to build self-esteem through external badges of merit and conspicuous consumption; we will feel more alive, connected with, and sensitive to our environment, whether human or otherwise; we will embrace life rather than trying to escape it through increasingly extreme forms of distraction or mind numbing. Knowing ourselves and our universe, we will be far less susceptible to manipulation. We will begin to realize our potential as human beings and demonstrate it to our children.

Transforming ourselves individually will automatically transform our planet (in ways that will be discussed further in chapter five). We will make different consumer decisions, elect different political leaders, set different communal priorities, and conduct our lives differently, day to day, whether we are farmers, accountants, garbage workers, teachers, scientists, parents, or brain surgeons. Transformation will ricochet backwards and forwards through all four "quadrants" of our lives. The great suffering, destruction, disease, brutality, and killing due to war will diminish.

The individual's potential and innate connection with society was described 2500 years ago, in the Chinese classic, *Dao De Jing*:

> Without going out of the door
> One can know the whole world;
> Without peeping out of the window
> One can see the Tao of heaven.
> The further one travels
> The less one knows.
> Therefore the sage knows everything without traveling;
> He names everything without seeing it;
> He accomplishes everything without doing it.

CHAPTER 3

THE AGELESS WISDOM:

OUR COMMON GROUND

The reader may be wondering, if Ageless Wisdom spirituality is so profound and common to so many cultures, why the average person knows so little about it. It is a question that I myself have pondered and is certainly relevant to the notion that the Ageless Wisdom may hold the key to the urgently needed shift in human consciousness. Over the long term, it might be argued that the mass of human consciousness (not counting a few exceptional individuals) has hitherto not evolved to a high enough level to appreciate it. One of the main questions this book explores is whether we have finally reach that level and if so, how can we facilitate bringing this knowledge forward.

In considering the state of spirituality now, one of the main obstacles to the spreading of the Ageless Wisdom is ironically spirituality itself, or more precisely, the overwhelming dominance of popular Christianity and Islam. Most people seem ignorant of the fact that these two religions not only share the same Semitic roots and line of prophets but also a similar appetite for conquest and conversion. In the 800 years following Muhammad's death in 632 CE, Islamic armies took Islam as far west as Spain, as far east as India and China and south into Africa. From about 1500 CE onwards, it was Christianity's turn. The European Christians used their powerful navies to aggressively (and at times, brutally) colonize the planet, imposing their religion, science and technology on all cultures. As a result, more than half of the world's current population of six billion is either Christian (nearly two billion) or Islamic (over one billion).

The sheer numbers of these two religions, together with the dominance of North American/ European culture have created the illusion that they cover most of the religious and spiritual spectrum. Indeed, it is still common for major American TV networks, in broad religious discussions, to feature representatives of just Judaism, Christianity and Islam, with the latter billed as representing the "eastern" perspective. All three are actually part of the same religion, which is most definitely western. Such discussions thus yield slightly different reflections of the same religious face. Truly eastern religions like Hinduism (0.8 billion), Buddhism (0.4 billion) often get no chance to put forward their perspective. There are actually more Daoists (20 million) than Jews (15 million) today.

Another factor that helps sustain this ignorance is postmodernism. It is considered politically incorrect, as we have seen, to suggest that a certain spiritual practice (or indeed any perspective) is qualitatively more advanced or sophisticated than another. Thus, for example, many textbooks and media representatives will accurately describe the slaughters that took place in the name of religion but not question it in any way (especially if it involves Christianity or Islam) for fear of being thought "judgmental". Conquest is not a necessary aspect of religion as Buddhism, Hinduism and Daoism (among others) demonstrate. Interfaith discussions, in which I have often participated, are reduced to the trite and polite: "We should all love each other." Yes, we should but we do not and there are reasons why.

In the Ageless Wisdom, there is not much danger of setting one race or country against another, because it advocates internal transformation rather than the filling of designated holy meeting places and their coffers. Moreover, mystic sects, generally recognized as part of the Ageless Wisdom, are to be found in most of the major religions, eastern and western. The *Concise Oxford Dictionary* defines "mystic" as a "person who seeks by contemplation and self-surrender to obtain unity or identity with or absorption into the Deity or the ultimate reality; mysterious and awe-inspiring." Perhaps, therein lie more reasons for its obscurity—no rousing messiahs or prophets promising the certainty of righteousness now and heavenly rewards later, just the seemingly boring and anti-social prospect of introspection, self-surrender, compassion and wisdom.

The Impact of Genesis

Whether we realize it or not, most people in the Judeo-Christian West (which exports its culture globally) as well as in the Islamic world get their ideas about the human being's place in the world from the Bible's Book of Genesis "creation story." This describes not only the creation of the universe and this planet, but of the first humans, Adam and Eve, in their idyllic Garden of Eden. As is also well known, this paradise was lost because of the temptation of these original humans and they were expelled from Eden. We do not have to attend a church, mosque or synagogue to receive these ideas for they are etched into the very fabric of our culture and society.

A selective summary of this story is as follows: After the Lord God made the heavens and the earth, he formed the first human, Adam, out of dust from the earth—adamah, literally means "dust from the soil." He then breathed life into Adam's nostrils and set him in the idyllic Garden of Eden. God told Adam he could eat from any tree in the beautiful and bountiful garden, except from the Tree of Knowledge, "for in the day that thou eatest thereof, thou shalt surely die." Subsequently, in order to find a fit companion for Adam, he caused him to fall into a deep sleep, took one of his ribs, and used it to create Eve, the first woman.

In time, the subtle and sly Serpent approached Eve and encouraged her to eat of the fruit of the Tree of Knowledge, promising her she would not die, but that her eyes would be opened and she would be like a god, knowing good and evil. She ate the fruit, realized that she had not died, and then took the fruit of the Tree of Knowledge to Adam and persuaded him to eat it as she had done. Having eaten the fruit, they immediately acquired knowledge of good and evil and indeed of all contrasting opposites. They realized that they were naked and for the first time feeling shame, they made aprons to cover their naked bodies. The Lord God not surprisingly found out what had happened and cursed the Serpent, putting enmity between the Woman's seed and the Serpent's seed. He then promised to increase the Woman's sorrow (since she had seduced Adam) by decreeing that she would give birth to children and be under the rule of her husband. Adam and Eve would henceforth have to work for their survival, and they would become mortal, eventually returning to the dust from whence they came. The Lord God then declared, "Behold, the man is become one of us to know good and evil; and now lest he put forth his hand and also take from the Tree of Life, and eat, and live forever. Therefore the Lord God sent him forth from the Garden of Eden."

Regardless of the intentions of the original tellers of this creation story, the holy books of the Western religions have long been and still are widely treated as literal accounts of the acts and words of the one and only God and subsequently of his chosen prophets and peoples.

It is clear from the above, the Lord God is regarded as the Supreme Creator and ruler. Humanity is but a part of the creation process, having been fashioned from mere dust. The Creator and the Creation are therefore not the same in essence. Evil originated not from God but from Adam and Eve (with the help of the diabolical Serpent), who disobeyed his commands and were subsequently expelled from the garden and cursed with what we now experience as everyday life—knowledge, working, having children, getting sick, aging, and dying. One of the main lessons literalists take from this creation story is that it is not wise to disobey God's words and rules, even though they may seem arbitrary and may change over time. A substantial shadow was also cast over the issue of sexuality because of Eve's interactions with the "serpent," her temptation and seduction of Adam, etc. Guilt is not limited to sexuality but is generalized because of Adam's and Eve's original sin. The feeling that we must always work harder to improve ourselves so that we can be worthy of salvation and heaven is still with us in the concept of ongoing "progress."

Some problematic questions are generated by a literal interpretation of the Genesis creation story. For instance, if God created everything in the universe including humans, who were in turn responsible for original sin and evil, did God not (albeit indirectly) create evil? Did God not create the Devil, and if so, for what reason? Should God, being omniscient, not have known that this temptation and fall would happen? How was the Serpent able to talk and why did it seem to know more than the humans who were made in God's image? Why was it a bad thing for Adam and Eve to eat from the Tree of Knowledge, get to know good and evil and thus become "as gods"? Why did they not die after eating the fruit from the Tree of Knowledge as God had threatened? Was Adam as originally made in God's image (before Eve) a male as we now define it or a self-sufficient hermaphrodite? How does this reconcile with the theory of evolution, carbon dating, etc., which show the world to be much older than the literal interpretation of the Bible and strongly suggest that humans evolved from apes. Feminists have been particularly incensed (at men, the church, hierarchy, etc.) because of the notions that Woman, or Eve, was formed from Man, that she was portrayed as a weak, gullible temptress, that she was put under the rule of her husband, and that giving birth to children was regarded as a punishment.

Many scholars, thinkers, writers, and teachers regard the book of Genesis as just one (albeit extremely influential) version of a myth or parable that arose in the Middle East. Certain symbolism in the myth like the Tree and the Serpent were very ancient, but the idea of a creation, fall, and restoration was probably only a few hundred years older than the book of Genesis and has been attributed to the Persian prophet, Zoroaster, who has been dated as early as 1500 BCE.

Joseph Campbell, in his *Occidental Mythology*, stressed the immense impact of Zoroaster's ideas on Western thought and attitudes down the millennia and the fact that it constituted a significant departure from existing mythology:

> Two contrary powers made and maintain the world in which men live: first, Ahura Mazda, the Lord of Life, Wisdom and light, Creator of the Righteous Order; but then, too, his antagonist, Angra Mainyu, the Demon of the Lie, who when the world had been made, corrupted every particle of its being. These two powers are coeval; for they have existed from all eternity. However, both are not eternal, for the Demon of the Lie is to be undone at the end of time, when truth alone will prevail. Thus we note beside the primary novelty of the ethical posture of the Zoroastrian system, a second novelty in its progressive view of cosmic history. This is not the old, ever-revolving cycle of the archaic Bronze Age mythologies, but a sequence, once and for all, of creation, fall and progressive redemption, to culminate in a final, decisive, irrefragable victory of the One Eternal God of Righteousness and Truth.

It was astonishing to me to hear both President George W. Bush and Osama bin Laden describe their conflict in ancient Zoroastrian terms as a cosmic battle between good and evil. Each of course thought he represented the "good."

What and Where Is Spirit?

The Ageless Wisdom spiritual traditions, in contrast to popular religion, do not regard the Supreme Deity or Absolute Spirit as separate from its creation, whether human, animal, vegetable, or mineral. What in the West has been called the "creation" process is in the Ageless Wisdom seen as "involution"—a voluntary descent of the one Spirit into dense, fragmented matter, which causes Spirit, thus embedded, to lose consciousness (be in the dark) regarding its true nature.

The involution process is always followed by one of evolution and this cycle is repeated over endless eons. As we evolve, becoming more complex and capable on the physical level, so the light of our consciousness and awareness becomes stronger and more widespread, illuminating the dark. For humans, this process does not stop at the level of well-balanced individuality (our present general level) but grows beyond, until the individual can fully realize his or her true nature as pure Spirit, at one not only with all humans but also with all manifestation. This process has been described as "Enlightenment" and in terms of broad human history, may take many thousands of years. In his book, *The Supreme Identity*, Alan Watts observed:

> The story of "lost and found," of death and resurrection, of
> self-forgetting and self-discovery, is perhaps the most
> common theme of mythological and religious symbolism.

In the Perennial /Ageless Wisdom traditions, God, Spirit, Dao, Brahman, or the Absolute, is not a supreme, personalized, humanlike being with astounding powers, but the Ground of all Being. Spirit is equally present in all manifestation, including all people regardless of their race or religion and in all "lower" life forms. Thus, we are all expressions of the absolute Spirit right now, and in that sense we are all right! Yet at the same time, Spirit is the very summit of being and is beyond (not confined to) manifestation, time, and space. We generally still have much spiritual work to do in transforming our consciousness before we can be consistently conscious of our true spiritual nature. Even being aware of this potential, however, can be inspiring and can give us clearer direction and perspective in how to conduct our individual and collective lives. If we understand this, for example, we would not be frantically seeking a technological Utopia because we would realize many of our seemingly external problems are actually generated within ourselves.

In more precise terms, it can be said that Spirit, the Absolute, the Supreme is both transcendent and immanent. "Transcendent" is defined in the dictionary as "(especially of the Supreme Being) existing apart from, not subject to the limitations of the material universe." "Immanent" is defined as "indwelling, inherent, (of the Supreme Being) permanently pervading the universe."

The sacred (Brihadaranyaka) Upanishad of India, dated 1000-700 BCE or roughly the same era as Zoroaster, states:

> The World existed first as seed, which as it grew and developed took on names and forms. As a razor in its case or as fire in wood, so dwells the Self, the Lord of the Universe, in all forms, even to the tips of the fingers. Yet the ignorant do not know him, for behind the names and forms he remains hidden.

The (Isha) Upanishad advises:

> The Self is one. Unmoving, it moves swifter than thought. The senses do not overtake it, for it always goes before. Remaining still, it outstrips all that run. Without the Self, there is no life . . . . He who sees all beings in the Self and the Self in all beings hates none. To the illumined soul, the Self is all. For him who sees everywhere oneness, how can there be delusions or grief?

A similar view is found in the Chinese Classic, *Dao De Jing* (The Way and its Power,) which is generally attributed to the legendary sixth century BCE patriarch of Daoism, Lao Zi. Its opening lines are:

> The Dao that can be expressed is not the eternal Dao;
> The name that can be defined is not the unchanging name.
> Non-existence is called the antecedent of heaven and earth;
> Existence is the mother of all things.
> From eternal non-existence therefore, we serenely observe
>   the beginning of the Universe;
> From eternal existence we clearly see the apparent distinctions.
> The two are the same in source and become different when
>   manifested.

The Dao is all that is, whether seen as *Wuji*, primordial Emptiness or non-existence, or as *Taiji* (Tai Chi,) the interplay of the manifested opposites of *Yin* and *Yang* that arise out of *Wuji*. In this sense, the Dao is very much like the Hindu greater "Self," as opposed to the small individual "self."

Such ideas never attained the widespread and lasting influence in the West as they did in the East. There were, however, always flames, sometimes faint and flickering, sometimes burning bright, that kept the mystic and Perennial Wisdom fires alive in the West. The earliest and perhaps most important influences on Western mysticism were the mystery schools and great sages of Greece, including Socrates and Plato, and a few centuries later (third century CE), the neo-Platonist, Plotinus, who wrote thusly of the ultimate reality, the One:

> If we are to think positively about the One, there would be more truth in silence . . . (the One) is Everything and Nothing; it can be none of the existing things, and yet it is all.

A hundred years before Plotinus, the mystic Gnostic sect of Christianity was at its height and has been an influence on Western mystics down the centuries.

Perhaps the greatest flowering of mysticism within the Western religions took place during the thirteenth century. The mystic Islamic sect of Sufism was at its peak, inspired by Rumi, the great Sufi saint, poet, and founder of the "Whirling Dervishes." During the same period, the mystical Jewish work, the *Zohar*, was being written in Spain and it subsequently became the most influential text among the growing number of Kabbalists. The mystical sect of Christian Cathars was strong in the south of France, and Meister Eckhart was starting to teach in Germany.

Much of the early impetus for this cross-pollination of mysticism came from the Sufis. The Arabs had captured Spain and their culture and ideas began to spread across Europe. Spain moreover became a refuge for a growing number of Jews who were being persecuted by Christians throughout Europe. Scholars have detected the influence of earlier Western mystics like the Gnostics and the Neoplatonists in these later mystic movements.

Karen Armstrong, a former Roman Catholic nun and author of the best-seller, *A History of God*, writes of the impact of the mystics on mainstream Western religion:

> Judaism, Christianity and to a lesser extent, Islam have all developed the idea of a personal God, so we tend to think that this ideal represents religion at its best. The personal God helps monotheists to value the sacred and inalienable rights of the individual and to cultivate an appreciation of human personality . . . Yet a personal God can become a grave liability. He can be a mere idol carved in our own image, a projection of our limited needs, fears and desires. We assume that he loves what we love and hates what we hate, endorsing our prejudices instead of compelling us to transcend them . . . .

All three of the monotheistic religions (Judaism, Christianity and Islam) developed a mystical tradition, which made their God transcend the personal category and become more similar to the impersonal realities of nirvana and Brahman-Atman.

Shortly after this mystic flowering, the rise of modern science turned the Christian gaze firmly towards the material world. As Christian Europe and subsequently America grew more powerful, the rest of the world was increasingly drawn into this new way of looking at ourselves, our planet, and God.

The Problem of the Separate "I" or Self

The most immediate problem we encounter in trying to grasp the idea that "God and I are the same" is that it seems to contradict down-to-earth "reality." For most people, it seems "obvious" that we are separate, fragile, and mortal beings who are born and will die. How can we possibly be as god? We feel if we do not protect and look out for ourselves and our own "kind" (however defined), others might take advantage of us or even kill us. We know that there are ways whereby we can manipulate the physical world (including other people), and we try to use that to our advantage. We can point to history and past experience to support this "commonsense" approach.

All of the above may be accurate observations of life as we see it, but they may not comprise the complete picture—parts of the proverbial elephant but not the whole. There are several reasons for looking beyond our conventional perspective. Collectively, we need a significantly higher level of cooperation and sense of unity in order to tackle our pressing global problems—the environment, technology, terrorism, conflict, inequality, poverty and more. Lack of action may be catastrophic, especially for our children and their children. On the personal level, the spur to spiritual inquiry may be some personal tragedy—health, relationship, job, etc.—or the simple fact that in spite of our success and material possessions, we still lack fulfillment, meaning and purpose.

Several eminent philosophers and spiritual teachers over the ages have advised that one of the most fundamental questions we need to ask is, "Who am I?" We are flooded with impulses, feelings, thoughts, and desires, which we generally obey (subject to external restrictions), but we are mostly ignorant of whence or why these arise in our consciousness. This ignorance concerning the "I" that directs all our activity causes immense suffering to ourselves and others. The consequences of that fundamental ignorance will grow apace with the power of our technology. More powerful technology cannot fix it, only magnify its effects.

The answer to the question, "Who am I?" would impact in turn on all of the other great questions in our lives: "How should I live life?" "What is right and wrong?" "How can I find happiness?" "Is there a God, and if so, what is God's nature and relationship to me?" "What is the purpose in life?" "What happens after death?" etc.

Our present sense of a mental, egoic "I" is the result of the evolution of consciousness. Becoming aware of ourselves as separate, individual, thinking entities was a big evolutionary step forward for humanity, endowing us with immense power—hence perhaps the Genesis account of Adam and Eve eating from the Tree of Knowledge and becoming "as gods." Amazingly, we can witness this evolution of consciousness being reenacted in accelerated fashion in our own children (similar to the way a growing fetus reenacts our physical evolution) as they grow from helpless, newborn babes, unable to differentiate themselves from their physical surroundings, to toddlers, children, teenagers, and eventually adults. At each new stage, there is greater awareness of the world and the sense of what constitutes the "self" continues to expand.

The mature intellectual mind enables us to study the external world and manipulate it for our own ends. Our actions can be inappropriate and destructive, however, because we generally spend very little time looking inside. We have awesome mental tools but only a limited idea of who is wielding them or what is really behind our impulses and our often contorted schemes. In this sense, the "I" can be a dangerous blind spot in our consciousness, observing everything but itself.

Individuality is powerful, but it usually entails a sense of separation, both in space (from God, nature, others) and in time, from the past and the future. As soon as we are born, death becomes inevitable; whatever we gain, we immediately risk losing. We cannot have the good without the bad because they are part of the same process. The more the thinking mind analyzes and tries to control, the more fragments of life (and complexity) are generated. The process of fragmentation and alienation takes place both externally and internally. Although these processes are now manifesting in a world of concrete, glass, and modern technology, they were recognized long ago by the great sages. Over 2,500 years ago, Lao Zi observed in the *Dao De Jing*:

> Dao begets One; one begets two; two begets three; three begets all things. All things are backed by the shade (yin) and faced by the light (yang) and harmonized by the immaterial breath (qi) . . . .

When all in the world understand beauty to be beautiful,
then ugliness exists.
When all understand goodness to be good, then evil exists.
Thus existence suggests non-existence;
Easy gives rise to difficult.

In modern terminology, Lao Zi is talking about our relationship with the ground of our being (God/Spirit/the Absolute) and the dynamics of change and complexity, including the constant interplay of seemingly opposite forces, which the Chinese term Yin and Yang. In my own experience, Lao Zi's words of wisdom work at all levels, whether applied to physical activities and interaction, interpersonal and group (including international) relationships, the health of the mind-body system or higher spiritual practice.

At about the same time of Lao Zi's *Dao De Jing*, one of the world's greatest Ageless Wisdom teachers, the Buddha, was teaching in India. The question which spurred him on his spiritual quest and which was the focus of his lifelong teaching (forty-five years, following his enlightenment) is precisely the one we have been discussing—how can an individual, if at all, overcome the pain and suffering that inevitably comes with living? The Buddha's teachings explored human internal dynamics in a way people today, with the benefit of modern psychology, can more readily understand.

Siddhartha Gautama was born around 563 BCE in Northern India, near Nepal, as the son of a local king. At his birth, a fortuneteller predicted that if he remained engrossed in everyday affairs, he would become a conqueror and one of India's greatest kings. If he forsook the world, however, he would be a world redeemer, savior, and teacher. In an attempt to keep his son interested in worldly affairs, the king shielded him from ugliness and unpleasantness and kept him entertained and distracted within the artificial world of the royal family's luxurious pleasure palaces. He was a very handsome man and married a beautiful princess. In short, he lived the type of life that many of us, even in the more privileged countries of our present world, still desperately seek.

Legend has it that curiosity and restlessness got the better of him, and he started making secret trips outside the palace to see what ordinary life was like. He was shocked and disillusioned to discover the existence of sickness, old age, and death, and the realization that every person was subject to these inevitabilities. Soon after this discovery, around the age of 29, he left his wife and newborn child in the palace, shaved his head, dressed in rags, and started wandering throughout India to search for the truth. He spent 6 years on his quest, studying with teachers of various spiritual paths and, in the process, subjecting himself to extreme ascetic practices and deprivation, almost dying of starvation.

As a result of these experiences, he discovered the Middle Way, between the extremes of self-mortification and indulgence. He then made a vow to sit in meditation under what later became known as the "Bodhi Tree" until he achieved Enlightenment. He underwent a series of tests/attacks by the God of Desire and the Lord of Death (similar to Jesus' later temptations) before he attained his goal. The name Buddha means the Enlightened or Awakened one. He had come to fully realize that his true nature, in common with all other beings, was Spirit itself, which as we have seen, is both immanent and transcendent.

Knowing himself at such a profound level, he also knew other human beings, animals, and all manifestations of nature. Zen master Dr. D.T. Suzuki (1869-1966) wrote in his *Essays in Zen Buddhism*:

> The term "Buddha," "The Enlightened One," was of his own making. If a man understands what enlightenment is or really experiences it in himself, he knows the whole secret of the Buddha's superhuman nature and with it the riddle of life and the world. The essence of Buddhism must then lie in the Doctrine of Perfect Enlightenment.

The Buddha summarized his teachings in the Four Noble Truths. The First Noble Truth is that life is "Dukkha" (in the Pali language). Its most usual meaning is "suffering," but it also has connotations of impermanence and insubstantiality. Many people today stop inquiring further into Buddhism after hearing "suffering" and "pain." They dismiss it as "pessimistic," "negative," "gloomy," etc. This is ironic because the tendency (particularly pronounced in the West) to routinely categorize things as rigidly good or bad is precisely what, according to the Buddha, helps create and prolong suffering.

If we can inquire past this knee-jerk reaction, however, it is difficult to deny the fact of impermanence and its connection with suffering. Impermanence manifests even in relatively static, traditional societies but is impossible to ignore in our current era of rapid change. As we have seen, The Buddha was particularly struck by the facts of sickness, old age, and death, all of which still terrify us. It should be obvious that all relationships are subject to change and impermanence, including those with lovers, friends, spouses, parents, children, employers, employees, customers, etc. How much pain in relationship is caused not by conscious malice or wrongdoing but merely because the relationship is no longer as it once was? In other words, we have suffered merely because life has changed and we want to hold on to the past!

In our present high-tech era, the rate and scope of change is greatly accelerated. Social and moral codes are in constant flux; it is increasingly difficult to sustain the traditional family unit or even a long-term relationship; technological innovation is rapidly decreasing job security and opportunity as well as transforming the way we live. "Higher" material standards of living and medical care bring their own new afflictions like stress, cancer, heart attacks, obesity, addictions, AIDS, allergies, and the long-term warehousing of the aged, many of whom would have died a long time ago if it were not for advances in medicine.

With the current worship of youth, aging (the undeniable reminder of impermanence) is becoming an affliction rather than a natural stage of life. Warhol's prediction of "Fifteen Minutes of Fame" for everyone is a recognition of and a jaundiced "solution" to the fact of impermanence and insubstantiality. Early in the twentieth century, science began to recognize the fact of constant change and lack of solidity at the atomic and subatomic levels, but this does not seem to have changed our everyday conception of the universe as a collection of independent, solid objects that occasionally crash into each other. It is still common, although illogical, to regard change as some form of unjust and painful aberration.

The Second Noble Truth is "Samudaya" which is the source or arising of Dukkha. The most immediate cause of Dukkha is "Tanha," which has been variously translated as thirst, desire, craving, or attachment. This desire can be for anything—sense-pleasure, wealth, power, fame, a person, self-image, youth, beauty, ideas, beliefs, existence, becoming (something or someone), and even for non-existence. As the First Noble Truth points out, however, life is constantly changing, and there is nothing solid that we can hold. Thus we spend our lives in a frantic, futile battle against both life and ourselves, constantly struggling to grasp what is pleasurable or "good" and running away from what is "bad," undesirable, or painful. Even those fortunate enough to have reached their main goals or to have been blessed by inherited talent, beauty, or wealth, subsequently face the prospect of losing what they have—of being or having less (a "has been"), of old age, sickness, and death.

It should be noted that the things we desire and experience are not inherently "bad" or "sinful," but it is the attachment and clinging (often addiction) to them that causes us pain and suffering. We can quite naturally admire a beautiful rose, but we do not necessarily have to pick it and put it in vase, press it between the pages of a book or research ways to clone it. More often than not, our desires, attachments, and struggles set in motion chains of cause and effect (karma) that embroil our lives even more. We consequently feel victimized by fate, ignorant of the fact that we have largely created the circumstances of our lives in specific ways by our own actions and thoughts.

The Buddha's Third Noble Truth is that we can be liberated from our suffering through the cessation of "Dukkha," which is no less than the state of "Nirvana." Walpola Rahula tries to explain Nirvana in his book, *What the Buddha Taught*:

It can never be answered completely and satisfactorily in words, because human language is too poor to express the real nature of the Absolute Truth or Ultimate Reality which is Nirvana . . . just as the fish had no words in his vocabulary to express the nature of the solid land . . .

If Nirvana is to be expressed and explained in positive terms, we are likely to immediately grasp an idea associated with those terms, which may be quite the contrary. Therefore it is expressed in negative terms—a less dangerous mode perhaps . . . such negative terms as Tanhakkhaya, "Extinction of Thirst," Asamkhata, "Uncompound," "Unconditioned," Viraga, "Absence of Desire," Nirodha, "Cessation," Nibbana, "Blowing out" or "Extinction."

How can we eliminate "Dukkha"? The Fourth Noble Truth, also known as the Noble Eightfold Path, describes the moral guidelines and meditation practices necessary to accomplish this— right understanding, right thought, right speech, right action, right livelihood, right effort, right mindfulness, and right concentration.

"Dukkha" will cease if we remove one of its major causes, which is "Tanha"—craving, thirst, and attachment. The source of one's action then shifts away from the conditioned "I" or Ego. There is action, but it does not emanate from the "I." What is appropriate, through clear insight into what really is, in each moment, is simply done without attachment to the consequences of that action. There is doing but not necessarily a doer. Walpola Rahula writes:

According to Buddhism, the Absolute Truth is that there is nothing absolute in the world, that everything is relative, conditioned and impermanent . . . to see things as they really are (yathabhutam) without illusion or ignorance (avijja) is the extinction of craving thirst (tanhakkhaya) and the cessation (nirodha) of dukkha, which is Nirvana . . . . It is incorrect to think that Nirvana is the natural result of the extinction of craving. Nirvana is not the result of anything.

If it would be a result, then it would be an effect produced by a cause. It would be samkhata, "produced" and "conditioned" . . . Truth is. Nirvana is. The only thing you can do is to see it, to realize it.

Thai Vipassana meditation master Dhiravamsa writes on the same subject in *The Way of Non-attachment*:

People sometimes think of Buddhism as a negative religion because renunciation and equanimity appear dull and boring, but when we can let go without turning away, we find the secret of joy and love. Energy springs up, which is not exhausted by clinging and defending but is expressed in even proportions, in choiceless awareness and caring. The self loses its grip, we become content within insecurity, and our lives become a natural meditation upon whatever is.

I have so far featured Buddhism in this section because the Buddha focused on the "how to" of individual liberation. He purposely stayed away from speculative metaphysical discussion because he felt that this distracted from the task at hand— liberation. He likened this distraction to a man shot with a poisoned arrow, who then begins to speculate on the particulars of the arrow and the person who shot him rather than simply pulling out the arrow.

Other Ageless Wisdom teachings are consistent with the Buddha's. One of the most revered works in Hinduism, the Bhagavad Gita tells us:

He who seeth inaction in action and action in inaction, he is wise among men, he is harmonious, even while performing all action. Whose works are free from the mouldings of all desire, whose actions are burned up by the fire of wisdom, him the wise have called a sage. Having abandoned attachment to the fruit of action, always content, nowhere seeking refuge, he is not doing anything, although doing actions.

Huston Smith, in his popular book, *The World's Religions*, describes the mystic Sufis' concept of the separate self and contrasts it with the mainstream Islamic attitude:

> Because your existence is a standing out from something, which in this case is God, existence involves separation. To avoid it Sufis developed their doctrine of fana—extinction— as the logical term of their quest. Not that their consciousness was to be extinguished. It was their self-consciousness of themselves as separate selves replete with personal agendas— that was to be ended. If the ending was complete, when they looked inside the dry shells of their now-emptied selves they would find nothing but God. A Christian mystic put this point by writing, "God, whose boundless love and joy are present everywhere; He cannot come to visit you unless you are not there." (Angelus Silesius) . . . . The Sufis tightened the creedal assertion, "There is no god but God" to read, "There is nothing but God." To exoteric Muslims this sounded silly if not blasphemous.

In the above passages we must distinguish non-attachment from detachment, denial, and suppression, all of which eventually cause reaction. "Non-attachment" does not mean doing nothing or caring about nothing. Indeed, because the source of our action is immensely broadened (not limited to the small, personal self), it becomes more appropriate, effective, expansive, compassionate, and harmonious. What is done is in a sense non-action, yet at the same time, total action, because we are liberated from our fear of failure and disapproval, our rigid beliefs and superstition etc., and can optimally use all our tools and faculties. As is often illustrated in the performance of exceptional athletes, such an attitude of living life moment by moment can bring results far in excess of "psyching ourselves up" and "busting a gut."

In the context of the above, we must also differentiate between enlightenment and fanatical belief. On the surface, both may display complete conviction, but the former is characterized by the profound wisdom and universal compassion that comes with the direct realization that everything is part of the One. Fanatics often exhibit inflexibility, reaction, and violence because they are always defending their rigidly defined "truth" from the Other, the Enemy, etc. They are sometimes even willing to sacrifice their lives because life would be intolerably painful for them if their belief system is questioned or (unthinkably) overturned. For the enlightened person, there is no necessity for belief and defense of belief because life simply and clearly is.

The Evolution of Consciousness—Psychology, Psychics and Enlightenment

According to the Perennial Wisdom, everything we have been discussing in this chapter—the Genesis creation and fall, the problem of the "I" or separate self, etc.—can be seen as aspects of the evolution of consciousness. In the beginning, Spirit, Dao, God, Brahman, En Sof, Allah, Great Spirit, etc., descends into dense matter, thereby forgetting its true nature. At this point, consciousness is extremely dim. This process may be called "involution" since Spirit involves itself in gross, finite matter. Over time, matter, energy, and consciousness slowly begin to evolve or unfold and interact in an ever more complex manner. The light of consciousness increasingly illuminates the surrounding darkness. We are more aware of activity both in the "external" world as well as inside of ourselves. The completion of this evolutionary process, still far off for most of humanity, is the full recognition of one's true nature as Spirit itself—complete Enlightenment.

Alan Watts, in his book, *The Supreme Identity*, explains:

> From the successive standpoint of time, the drama of creation
> and redemption, of the infinite manifesting itself in the
> finite, may be divided into two stages. The first is involution,

> wherein the supreme Self deliberately forgets and lays aside
> its omniscience and identifies itself with finite points of
> view . . . the second is evolution, wherein the Self awakens
> to its true identity within the finite order, not forsaking it as
> a prison but using it as an instrument of expression.

There are many different maps or schemes, both ancient and modern, which describe the different levels of evolving human consciousness. For instance, the Western religions recognize body, mind, soul, and spirit; the Kabbalists study the various sefiroth (numerations) of divine reality; Theravada Buddhism recognizes the general human level (which has several sub-divisions) of Kamaloka (Pleasure-Pain) as well as those beyond the normal level of consciousness—Rupaloka (world of form), Arupaloka (formless worlds) and Lokuttara Citta (transcendental or supra-mundane consciousness).

The Hindu system of chakras is one of the oldest consciousness systems, yet quite similar (on the personal level) to modern psychological systems. The chakras serve not only as symbolic levels of consciousness but describe actual centers of energy (*prana*) in the body that impact on day-to-day health. The lower two chakras relate to the physical body—survival, sexuality, procreation, etc.; the middle two chakras govern the emotions and relationships; the upper two relate to speech, the intellectual mind, and intuition. The seventh chakra relates to the various transpersonal levels of consciousness. The Daoist system of the Three *Dan Tians* (fields of elixir) is very similar to the Six Chakras, both in function and location, except condensing every two levels into one.

Amazingly, many of the major maps of consciousness—Eastern and Western, ancient and modern—have been reconciled and shown to be largely consistent. Much of this work has been pioneered by Ken Wilber. This is an exciting and invaluable resource, because it plots in detail much of the common ground of the Ageless Wisdom traditions, providing us with a cross-cultural alternative to scientism and a well-researched way out of the postmodern morass. As we have seen from his "Four Quadrants" theory (described in chapter two), Wilber not only worked on personal maps of unfolding consciousness (from birth to adulthood), but he has linked them with the evolution of collective consciousness in various societies and cultures over the ages.

Wilber describes the importance of the "spectrum of consciousness" in his book *The Eye of the Spirit*:

> Not as well known, but arguably more important (than the Human Genome Project), is what we might call the Human Consciousness Project, the endeavor to map the entire spectrum of human consciousness (including as well, realms of the human unconscious) . . . . Involving hundreds of researchers from around the world, including a series of multidisciplinary, multicultural, multimodal approaches that together promise an exhaustive mapping of the entire range of consciousness . . . By comparing and contrasting various multicultural approaches—from Zen Buddhism to Western psychoanalysis, from Vedanta Hinduism to existential phenomenology, from Tundra Shamanism to altered states— these approaches are rapidly piecing together a master template.

I will hereunder attempt a brief summary (roughly based on Wilber's work) of the various levels of consciousness. The first six levels relate to individual/personal consciousness manifesting today and can be said to comprise the domain of most forms of modern psychology, i.e., how to be a balanced, secure, well-functioning individual within society.

Consciousness evolves by differentiating itself from its present level and moving to a higher, more complex level, which nevertheless includes the lower. This is similar to the process that occurs in our physical bodies as a cell evolves out of molecules, which in turn have evolved out of less complex atoms. If something goes wrong with the evolutionary consciousness process, a psychological disorder (relating to that particular level of consciousness) may result. Wilber's rule for successful evolution is "transcend and include."

Although this may seem obvious, human history is full of denial and demonization of what has gone before—the physical, sexual, instinctual, etc. At present, we can witness this process of suppression in those people who try to make the logical mind the only proper mode of functioning not only in themselves but also in others. Feeling smugly superior, they mock emotion, instinct, and intuition.

The first differentiation of consciousness within individuals occurs at about 4 months old when the infant begins to realize that she or he has a separate physical being, apart from the external environment. This is the Hindu "base" chakra level (which we carry with us as we mature), relating to physical survival, body comfort, and procreation. Historically, this level of consciousness characterized the very earliest human societies and is not seen as the main mode of consciousness in mature adults today except in the mentally ill or severely traumatized.

The next level of consciousness begins to unfold as the infant approaches her second year. She starts to differentiate from her emotional environment, which in most cases means the mother or any other major caregiver. At this stage, the infant often suffers separation anxieties as she struggles to set emotional boundaries. Before differentiation, life is magical and narcissistic since the whole world seems like an extension of the self. She imagines that the whole world is seeing, hearing, and feeling as she does. Societies at this level are tribal, given to superstitions, spells, and magic through which they feel they can control the world. Wilber estimates that this consciousness characterizes 10 percent of the present world population, wielding 1 percent of its power.

The beginning of the third level marks the emergence of the "representational" mind and the mental-conceptual self. Basic mental capacities slowly develop—language, the notion of past and future, symbols, and eventually concepts. This process starts at about 7 months old and continues to about 7 years. As the mind develops conceptually, it also becomes capable of repression and disassociation. At this stage, the self begins to realize that it cannot really control the world (through magic and spells) but thinks that there are powerful, mythic beings that can—gods, goddesses, etc., who may be swayed by prayer, ritual, and the like. This is the consciousness behind the frontier mentality, feudal kingdoms, and modern gangs. This consciousness accounts for 20 percent of present population and 5 percent of power in society.

The fourth level is the development of the "concrete operational" or "rule/role" mind, which takes place approximately between 7 and 14 years of age. The child learns to take the role of another person and is concerned with fitting in with her peer group, learning "right" and "wrong" behavior, what is "in" and "out," "cool," etc. Collectively, this kind of consciousness underlies early, ancient nation states and those today that tend to have rigid rules of right and wrong, stressing law and order. Fundamentalism is an obvious example of this category. This level of consciousness is reflected in 40 percent of the population and 30 percent of the power currently being exercised.

The fifth level occurs in individuals approximately between 11-15 years of age, when the now mature ego is capable of "formal operational" awareness, i.e., it can think about thought itself. It can now judge and criticize conventional rules and roles and ponder possibilities apart from what already exists. This new ability, together with growing independence and sexuality, often contributes to idealistic, teenage rebellion. Wilber discerns this level of development in those who see the world as consisting of predictable laws that can be mastered and controlled by the rational mind— scientific materialism, corporate states, Wall Street, the middle classes, secular humanism, liberal self-interest, etc. Wilber estimates that this consciousness operates in 30 percent of the population and 50 percent of the power-wielders.

The sixth level is the last orthodox or conventional stage of consciousness and is so broad in its range that some systems subdivide them into two or three distinct stages. At the beginning of this level, the self begins to realize that life is not so predictable as to always fall into "either-or" reasoning. It starts to recognize more complex interactions and processes taking place and that the fact that the individual self is not an island—it too is entangled in the web of life. This leads to a greater desire for communication, dialogue, networking, and a more global, multicultural perspective (at least in theory). Concern for the planet begins to grow.

All the above is of course healthy and positive, but as we saw in chapter one, development at this level can become diverted and stuck in aperspectivism (all perspectives are equal), political correctness, and pluralistic relativism. This reaction against any notion of hierarchy (i.e., that a thing may have more inherent quality and complexity than another) inflicts us with postmodern paralysis—the inability to make decisions or distinguish innate quality or value. Reassuring each other that "Everything and everyone is OK" and "You do your thing and I'll do mine" is very polite but does not resolve conflicts. It merely delays them and perhaps allows them to become more entangled. Wilber estimates this stage exists in about 10 percent of the population and accounts for approximately 15 percent of the power being exercised.

The evolution of consciousness beyond this point, according to Wilber, is rather rarified—less than 2 percent of the population, with only about 0.1 percent even entering into the transpersonal. This, I would guess is far less than the popular impression but is more or less in line with much earlier estimates by people like Carl Jung, who felt that the vast majority of the patients that he had successfully treated were in fact just starting (not completing) a journey of self-exploration and transformation.

In the later stages of the sixth level of consciousness, awareness becomes capable of ever more integration and synthesizing, of not only horizontal thinking, but vertical as well. It can begin to understand and accommodate interactions coming from levels of consciousness different from its own, rather than simply condemning them as wrong. The world is seen as dynamically complex, not only horizontally but also vertically, and yet at the same time integrated and connected.

This can be a frightening and depressing time because the self is beginning to realize that what the Buddha and the Hindu sages were saying over 2,500 years ago may actually be true—that the separate self is not actually a solid, "real" entity. It is one thing to develop new faculties while retaining the concept of the solid, individual self, but quite another to realize that the self itself may have to be left behind. The prospect of the death of the ego can be as terrifying as that of physical death. Perhaps in terms of the Garden of Eden, this amounts to the recognition that it may be necessary to make the long journey back from exile to the overwhelming presence of God.

When we begin to leave behind the old, amazing new possibilities begin to open up. The functions of the sixth or highest personal chakra, the Ajnachakra, are described by Vasant V. Merchant in the book, *Kundalini, Evolution and Enlightenment*:

> With the opening of this center and the force, there is opening of a greater will, power of decision, formation, effectiveness, beyond what the ordinary mind can achieve; bestows inner vision, sees inner forms and images of things and people from within and not only from outside. It is the beginning of the yogic as opposed to ordinary mental consciousness.

Before we discuss the transpersonal or transcendental levels of consciousness, it is well to note that within these first six levels, as the self differentiates itself from each successive level and rises to the next, consciousness correspondingly expands while egocentrism and narcissism decrease. The notion of the "self" expands beyond identification with the physical body, then the emotions and then thought. It continues to expand beyond the individual, the tribe and the nation until a global or planetary identity begins to form.

In both individuals and groups, the evolution of consciousness does not take place evenly. Thus within individuals, certain spheres of our lives may reflect greater development than others. Within society, certain individuals or groups may develop faster or slower than the average. Although this may largely explain different levels of capability in different spheres of life, it does not mean that certain individuals or groups are intrinsically stupid or inferior. If we are aware of the potentiality and nature of consciousness, there is much we can do to repair damage or speed up development at various levels. In addition to traditional spiritual disciplines, different fields of study, treatment, and education are springing up all the time.

In order to make room for transpersonal consciousness, we have to progressively let go of our attachments to and identification with the personal ego or "I." At this point, the Ageless Wisdom and conventional psychotherapy begin to part company. At the moment, not many psychotherapy clients (with the exception of those involved with transpersonal psychology) want to pay good money to be told they have to die to themselves and their past! The radical difference between boosting the ego to assertiveness and efficient functioning and dissolving the ego entirely is an important factor to consider for those claiming all truths and all forms of spirituality are the same. It should also be pointed out that letting go of attachment to the "I" does not mean that the "I" cannot function in everyday life. Ironically, it may function more efficiently. This topic will be explored in the next chapter.

Wilber's research into the Perennial Wisdom traditions has led him to distinguish four ascending levels of transcendental consciousness that he terms Psychic, Subtle, Causal, and Ultimate or Non-dual. The term "enlightenment" may be generally taken to cover the higher end of this transcendental spectrum, depending on the context of the specific tradition and speaker or writer in question.

The Psychic level straddles the personal and the transpersonal. The Ajnachakra is still influential as consciousness begins to move beyond the confines of rational, scientific "reality." "Paranormal" events may more readily (but not necessarily) occur at the Psychic level and may include intuition, abnormal powers (*siddhis*), out-of-body experiences, shamanic trance, manipulation of emotional-sexual energy (*qi, prana*), hands-on healing, Qigong, Kundalini yoga, Hatha yoga, and the temporary dissolution between subject and object as the self becomes as one with the environment.

Psychic level consciousness is presently beginning to manifest within popular culture and is fascinating a growing number of people, as well it should. Three points, however, ought to be borne in mind. Firstly, this is just the leading edge—the first trickles—of a new level of consciousness, not the sign of a massive wave about to crash on us. Secondly, the Psychic is not the ultimate level of spirituality but only the first step into the transpersonal. Thirdly, those who exhibit psychic ability are not necessarily enlightened or even balanced individuals, since this requires balancing and integrating all the "lower" levels we have been discussing. Indeed emotional volatility may sometimes open a door into the Psychic level.

We are all able to access Spirit (have a "peak" experience) at various rungs of the consciousness ladder because Spirit is our very nature, but that does not mean that we cannot slip on a certain rung or that our personal ladder is not dire need of repair at various rungs. Even if we do have a peak experience, it does not mean that we are spiritually superior to others or that our subsequent life will be better. It all depends on what we learn from that experience and how we apply it in our lives. We may draw an erroneous conclusion from our experience or spend our whole lives trying to re-live that experience to the detriment of our ongoing spiritual practice.

The level of consciousness after the Psychic is the Subtle. Consciousness is beginning to differentiate from the ordinary mind and ordinary self and may start communicating or identifying with archetypal forms like angels or even God, which may be viewed as the highest archetype of the self. In his *Eye to Eye*, Wilber explains,

> The deep structure of this overall realm is simply that of archetypal form; it is marked by transmental illumination, intuition and beginning gnosis, which brings a profound insight into the fundamental or Archetypal forms of being and existence itself. It is not Formless, however, or radically transcendent, but rather expresses insight into the subtlest forms of mind, being, deity and manifestation.

Wilber includes in this level, Theravada Buddhism's Four Jnanas with Form, Vipassana's pari—or pseudo-Nirvana, Zen's absorption in one's koan, Mahayana's Sambhogakaya, the seventh chakra (sahasrara) in the Yoga system, the Platonic forms, halos of subtle light and sound. At this stage of consciousness, we may experience a temporary bridging of the gap between subject and object while the mind is in a state of trance or absorption.

At the Causal level, which succeeds the Subtle, transcendence becomes so complete and stabilized that there is no need for forms— even of the archetypal deity—to arise in consciousness. There is unity, emptiness, formlessness, and dissolution into one's own ground of being. At this stage, there is no self, no god, no sense of separation and duality. V.R. Dhiravamsa points out:

> All the archetypes and mythologies are mere symbols of various states of consciousness or energy patterns manifesting both within us and the external world. As symbols they are man-made things.

This level is Mahayana's Dharmakaya, Theravada's Formless Jnanas, Vipassana's nirvanic or formless state and Zen's/*Chan's* seventh and eight Ox-herding pictures—"Cow forgotten, man alone" and "Both cow and man out of sight" respectively. The latter is represented by just an empty circle. This empty circle also appears in Daoism and is called "Wuji," the state prior to "Taiji," which is the interaction of the manifest opposites of Yin and Yang. The empty circle in *Chan* is used to describe a higher part of the evolutionary (unfolding) process of consciousness while in Daoism, it is often used to describe part of the involutionary process (prior to manifestation), but in essence it is the same.

The Ultimate state of consciousness is the Non-dual, the identity that includes both manifest and unmanifest . . . consciousness as such. At this stage, there is no need to go away from the world because the observer and the observed, the extraordinary and the ordinary, are the same. According to the Buddhist Heart Sutra, "Form is not other than Emptiness and Emptiness is not other than Form."

This state is Mahayana's Svabhavikakaya, the Indian Brahaman-Atman and Ch'an's tenth and final Ox-herding picture, "Entering the City with Bliss-bestowing Hands." At this final stage, the completely enlightened and transcended person goes back to his village and lives the "ordinary" life without making a show of his lofty inner attainments:

> Barechested and barefooted, he comes out into the marketplace; daubed with mud and ashes, how broadly he smiles! There is no need for the miraculous power of the gods, for he touches and lo! The dead trees come into full bloom.

Although these quotations are taken from the East, similar accounts can be found in Western traditions. Karen Armstrong writes in her *A History of God*:

> Throughout history, men and women have experienced a dimension of spirit that seems to transcend the mundane world . . . . However we choose to interpret it, this human experience of transcendence has been a fact of life. Not everybody would regard it as divine. Buddhists would deny that their visions and insights are derived from a supernatural source; they see them as natural to humanity. All the major religions, however, would agree that it is impossible to describe this transcendence in normal conceptual language.

Joseph Campbell, in his *Creative Mythology*, summarizes the West's current options regarding religion and spirituality:

> Since there was no Garden of Eden, no Adam and Eve, no Fall, then what is all the talk about Redemption unless by "Fall" and "Redemption" the same psychological states of ignorance and illumination are meant that the Hindus and Buddhist also are talking about? In which case, what happens to the doctrine of the unique historical importance of the

Incarnation and Crucifixion? The whole myth, to make any sense, must be totally reread . . . .

The functions of mythological symbols are four: mystic, cosmological, sociological and psychological; and today not only has science dissolved the claim of the Church and its Book to represent the second of these, the cosmological, but the social order once supposed to have been supported by scriptural authority also has dissolved. Even its social horizon has dissolved. The way in which India might contribute—and indeed already is contributing—to our rescue in this circumstance is through its teaching in the Upanishadic and Buddhist doctrines of the basically *psychological* origin, force and function of the same symbols that in our system have been read as a) revealed from a jealous personal God "out there" and b) historically unique.

CHAPTER 4

SPIRITUAL PATHS AND PITFALLS

Why Information and Reason Are Not Enough

If we, individually and collectively, accept the notion of and want to further the transformation and evolution of our consciousness, we would greatly benefit from the advice of those who have already explored that internal universe—the great Ageless Wisdom spiritual teachers.

One of the first stumbling blocks we encounter in this endeavor is that although we can hear and read about and even coherently discuss higher levels of consciousness, this is not the same as experiencing it or actually transforming our consciousness. Intellectual knowledge can easily lead us to overestimate our level of consciousness, and this indeed seems to be happening. Psychological studies suggest that the number of people who are actually entering or residing in the transpersonal levels of consciousness (less than one percent) is far smaller than the number of those who think they are. Both of these categories together are in turn miniscule in comparison to the number of those who are totally unaware of or dismiss the very possibility of higher consciousness.

The intellect-thinking and reasoning—presently is the predominant way of ordering our lives. Both psychological studies and "common sense" tell us so since we are required to use our thinking faculties in all aspects of our lives. We are trained to develop it throughout school and higher education; we are rewarded for it at work; it often determines our various kinds of relationships, even those intimate ones with significant emotional attachments. Thought not only shapes our individual lives but also impacts on our planet and beyond (satellites, space debris, interplanetary probes, etc.). As we have seen, for the vast majority of humanity, it is our latest and most powerful evolutionary tool and as such, it is eminently appropriate.

Not surprisingly, many people conclude that if we just had more of it, then all our problems would be solved. We have seen that high-profile scientists like Moravec and Kurzweil are already planning a robotic-genetic-nanotech future that may not need humans or even the planet. When the earth is completely exploited and spent, our robot descendents will leave and colonize some other planet. John Naisbitt gives a more current example of the way we overvalue knowledge:

> The most dangerous promise of technology is that it will make our children smarter. President Bill Clinton's 1996 State of the Union address proclaimed "the Internet in every classroom" to be a noble goal. Access to information will not teach synthesis and analysis. School expenditures on information technology reached $4.34 billion in 1997, yet at the same time programs for music and the arts were defunded.

Thinking is awesomely powerful, but it is not our ultimate tool or level of consciousness, and as should be obvious, it can be destructive as well as constructive. One of the common ways in which the intellect can go awry is when it overrules, misuses, or suppresses what it regards as "lower" faculties, or in Wilberian terms, when it transcends and represses rather than transcends and includes.

When we "live in our heads," we tend to lose touch with our other faculties, and thus behavior that should be natural and life enhancing can become distorted, debilitating, and life threatening.

In the West, for example, one of our most basic needs—food—has become a major health problem resulting in a wide variety of illnesses and disorders. Unlike the greater part of human history and even in many parts of the world today, however, the problem is not the lack of food but too much of it and the inappropriate types of it.

Instead of following our "gut instinct," we tend to follow what appeals to the head—what is sweeter or saltier, cheaper, more attractive, more fashionable, etc. Much of this in turn comes from those marketing the industry of eating, both in the private home and in restaurants. In spite of prevalent obesity, heart problems, and other related diseases, modern diets remain high in sugar, salt, fat, and a variety of doubtful additives. We pay more attention to the appearance of food (and its packaging) rather than to its nutritional value or what goes into it—pesticides, hormones, preservatives, and now genetic modification. Sometimes we eat to impress other people socially or to stifle emotions and boredom. What is essentially very simple, but nevertheless extremely important, becomes complex and puzzling because our natural instincts have been suppressed and distorted by our thinking minds.

Science is finally discovering and acknowledging what has long been obvious to many ordinary people—that there is intelligence throughout our being, not only within the brain. Television journalist Bill Moyers, in his book, *Healing and Mind*, interviewed Candace Pert, a professor at the Centre for Molecular and Behavioral Neuroscience at Rutgers University:

> We have sufficient scientific evidence to hypothesize that these information molecules, these peptides and receptors, are the biochemicals of emotions . . . they carry messages from the brain to the body, or from the body to the body or from the body to the brain. The old barriers between brain and body are breaking down . . . . In real life the brain and the immune system use so many of the same molecules to communicate with each other that we're beginning to see that the brain is not simply "up there."

If we take the time to examine ourselves and our society, it is not hard to find other examples of this intellectual tyranny and distortion. We have already seen how life-threatening stress arises from intellectual rigidity—in other words, from our unexamined conditioning and expectations. The issues of sex, sexuality, and gender are difficult to ignore because they now drive such a large part of our culture and society, especially advertising, entertainment, and media but also politics, law, etc. Biologically, the sexual impulse is driven by the instinct to procreate. This is now often subordinated to any number of fanciful and exploitative theories and motives, including power, profits, politics, which manifest not only in the bedroom but in society at large. Different kinds of sexual therapy are proliferating because the theoretical possibilities and disorders are endless. Often the afflicted organ is not really the sexual one but the thinking one.

Our intellectual tyranny, of course, extends to the external environment (right-hand quadrants). The whole planet is seen as fair game for all kinds of ill-conceived schemes—leveling of vast tracts of forest and jungle, scattering radioactive material throughout the atmosphere so that it is ingested by everyone on the planet, dumping poisons into the oceans, building luxurious palaces with waterfalls and lakes in the middle of deserts, altering the genetic structure of plants, animals, and humans without inquiring too deeply into possible wider consequences.

The solution to the runaway intellect is not to reject the thinking mind altogether and try to regress to some simpler (less evolved) state but to go forward, or in other words, transcend and include. We must learn how to integrate and balance the intellect with our other faculties and begin to explore what is beyond it . . . what can bring us the integration and harmony that are now so obviously lacking.

In this context, understanding the various stages of consciousness is important. It is easy to idealize some past state or period in time—innocence, magic, ritual—but we cannot go back to simple innocence because we are already complex. The hippies in the 1960s give it a spirited try but failed, and that failure in turn gave rise to the reactionary crassness of the 1980s and 1990s, which still haunts us. I am reminded of the story of the master trying to explain Enlightenment. He recounts that in the beginning, without any questioning or training, he would look at a mountain and think that a mountain is simply a mountain. Once he had embarked on his spiritual journey and was earnestly studying and meditating, he would look at a mountain and perceive all kinds of different possibilities and notions. A mountain was no longer simply a mountain. When he finally gained complete enlightenment, he would look at a mountain and remark, "A mountain is a mountain." Perhaps we are in the middle stage (of complexity and theorizing) and must go forward because we cannot go back, which is just another fanciful and complex notion.

Even if our intellect and ego are reasonably well balanced, there will still be problems as long as the source of our actions remains the separate "I." We will still struggle to maintain the solidity of something which is not solid, to hold on to that which is temporary, to defend our personal boundaries, and to maintain an identity which falls far short of its true state. The Buddha said that we suffer because we are attached, which is almost an automatic result of the mental-egoistic process. He did not say, "Be attached just enough to reap the money and the fame; be attached just enough to maintain the façade; be attached just enough to stay ahead of the next person."

If our actions emanate from the sense of an individual "I," that "I" has history. It is conditioned by past memories, feelings, and attitudes, which are activated in perpetual self-defense and self-promotion. Thought and information are enlisted in this ego-process and can be used to create or destroy any logical proposition. They also lead to increasing complexity, which further isolates and paralyzes us. The renowned spiritual teacher, J.D. Krishnamurti, wrote repeatedly about the dynamics of thought. Hereunder are a few excerpts from his *Commentaries on Living*:

> Independent thinking is a contradiction in terms. Thought,
> being a result, opposes or agrees, compares or adjusts,

condemns or justifies, and therefore it can never be free . . .
A result can never be free from its mooring. Thought is
anchored to memory.

Thought, with its emotional and sensational content, is not
love. Thought invariably denies love. Thought is founded
on memory and love is not memory . . . Thought inevitably
breeds the feeling of ownership, that possessiveness which
consciously or unconsciously cultivates jealousy. Where
jealousy is, obviously love is not . . . . It is thought that has
emotional complications, not love. Thought is the greatest
hindrance to love. Thought creates a division between what
is and what should be.

Belief, Conditioning, and the Separate Self

In this book so far, we have discussed the illusion of the separate
self, the need for a form of spirituality that goes beyond belief, and
why mere information and reason are not enough to take us to
Truth or Enlightenment. These issues are not only related but are
all part of the same process, which we may describe as
"conditioning".

Human beings operate somewhat like computers, which should
not be surprising, since computers were designed to imitate human
functioning. Most of us have strong opinions and convictions about
life based on what we have learned from our personal experiences,
formal academic and religious education, books, discussions and
increasingly from TV and the internet. We have experienced it so
we regard it as undoubtedly "true". We have confidence in the
"rightness" of our resulting words and actions, which in computer
terms, are our output.

We are (still) different from computers, however, in as much
as we have a sense of separate identity, self, ego or "I", which
identifies with and attaches to all the different parts, including
both hardware and software. The "I" becomes protective, fending
off criticism of its output and building defense mechanisms. A

very common mechanism is to reinforce belief systems by seeking out compatible experiences and like-minded believers. The stronger the belief, the more decisive and confident we feel and act, which often brings us success in the world. This in turn causes us to continue and expand our defensive strategy.

If instead of the above, the "I" were to inquire into and improve the accuracy of its input and processing, then the system's output would in turn be much more accurate and reflective of the wider world. The experiential input we each receive is quite individual (even among siblings) and has not been sorted to represent life as a whole. Distortions may be caused not only by accidents and trauma but more commonly and importantly by culture and society. Thus, people in a certain type of cultural environment will have the same general input, leading to the conclusion that it represents obvious "reality", but this will be different from the "reality" of other cultural and social environments.

Just as or perhaps even more important than input/ experience is our processing or computing unit, which has to interpret our experience. I have no doubt that we all have particular personality patterns, which are in place at birth or shortly thereafter. These predispose us to interpret life from specific perspectives. Personality may be viewed as our relationship vehicle, similar to the way that our body is our physical vehicle. They both have specific characteristics, which we may characterize as positive or negative and which we may alter to a certain extent. Apart from personality, our processing may be affected by certain "hardware" problems, which may be the result of faulty construction, limited capacity, lack of service and maintenance etc.

Most people would probably regard the above description of human functioning as too complex to bother about, preferring to believe as they do, "do their own thing" and others be damned. That is precisely the approach that has brought us to this point in time.

Belief and one-pointedness or single-mindedness are extremely powerful, but it is a mistake to confuse belief with wisdom or, in other words, to confuse power with the ability to guide it. In Buddhism, there is a clear distinction between the concentration and wisdom streams of meditation. We need the power of concentration to drive us towards Enlightenment but we can never get there without Wisdom to guide it. Thus, for example, we can rouse a mob (or a country) by focusing them on a certain idea or belief but the more zealous they become, the less clear thinking and open-minded they will be and the more difficult to control once aroused. We easily see this in others, but tend to think it cannot apply to us because we of course represent the "good" and "positive".

The interplay between belief and wisdom was evident shortly after the September 11 terrorist attacks. When some analysts started questioning whether American foreign policy over the years might somehow have contributed to the attacks, the Bush administration moved quickly to squash that line of thinking, declaring that America was in no way to blame and that to change American behavior in any way would be to show weakness and give in to terrorism. This was in line with Bush's challenge to the nations of the world, including friends and allies, "Either you're with us or you're with the terrorists." Bush's uncompromising position no doubt unified America in patriotic fervor and prepared it for war, since single-minded belief is indeed powerful. While this strategy worked in the short term to empower America, however, it also set it on a confrontational and unilateral course, which may have enormous repercussions long after Bush is a faded memory. I feel most of the world is eager to follow the lead of the U.S.A. but not at all costs, only if it displays the qualities it has touted to the world as the American Way—fairness, justice and caring for the downtrodden. This takes enormous wisdom and humility, including the greatness of heart to admit errors.

The other drawback with belief, of course, is when it comes up against an opposing and equally strong belief. In this way of thinking, the way to test which side God is really on is to go to war and see who wins. As history shows, however, neither belief nor military victory proves righteousness. As the power of our technology increases, this is an indulgence that may prove catastrophic to humanity.

The Buddha explained two and a half thousand years ago how and why we are conditioned and caught in the continuous cycle of becoming. His most detailed explanation is contained in the doctrine of *Paticca-samuppada*, which has been translated as "Conditioned Genesis" or "Dependent Origination." Many scholars regard this an elaboration of the dynamics explained in his Four Noble Truths. A short summary of this doctrine is given in four lines:

> When this is, that is;
> This arising, that arises;
> When this is not, that is not;
> This ceasing, that ceases.

In current parlance, we might say, "Nothing is absolute; everything is interdependent."

The complete doctrine of Dependent Origination lists twelve factors that give rise to each other and bind us to the Wheel of Becoming. The usual ordering of these conditioning factors is ignorance, volitional actions or "karma-formations," consciousness, mental and physical phenomena ("name and form"), the six sense faculties, contact, sensation or feeling, thirst or craving, clinging, becoming, rebirth, decay and death. Walpola Rahula in his *What the Buddha Taught*, comments on the *Paticca-samuppada* as follows:

> This is how life arises, exists and continues. If we take this formula in the reverse order, we come to the cessation of the process . . . It should clearly be remembered that each of these factors is conditioned as well as conditioning. Therefore they are all relative, interdependent and interconnected, and nothing is absolute and independent; hence no first cause is accepted by Buddhism as we have seen earlier . . . Free Will has occupied an important place in Western thought and philosophy. But according to Conditioned Genesis, this question does not and cannot arise in Buddhist philosophy. If the whole of existence is relative, conditioned and interdependent, how can Will alone be free?

Our thoughts and actions will be determined by our past conditioning unless we can find a way to transcend it or liberate ourselves from it. In this context, it must be noted that many people *want* to be bound by the past because it seems to give them a "solid and secure" identity—a sense of their history, shared beliefs and "roots." Accordingly, such people may be influenced by historical or even legendary events from hundreds or even thousands of years ago, even if it means provoking new wars now. As we have seen, on the personal level, rigidity of behavior also raises stress levels, especially in an era of accelerated change. To aptly respond to change, we must be flexible and capable of change.

As we have seen, the Buddha taught that we can stop the Wheel spinning through non-attachment or the cessation of craving. When J.D. Krishnamurti was asked how one could become aware of the process of conditioning, he too linked conditioning with attachment:

> It is possible only by understanding another process—the process of attachment . . . The object of attachment offers me the means of escape from my own emptiness. Attachment is escape and it is escape that strengthens conditioning. If I am attached to you, it is because you have become the means of escape from myself; therefore you are important to me and I must possess you . . . You become the conditioning factor and escape is the conditioning.

Wisdom: Beyond Progress, Pain, and Pleasure

How is it possible to live in a manner radically different from that which most of us experience—the compulsiveness of thought and desire (driven by the "I"), the feelings of separation, insufficiency and emptiness, the push-pull of the past and future, always wanting more and better, the grinding pressure of competition, stress and complexity, the sense of frustration and futility, and the fear of failure, inadequacy, sickness, old age, and eventually death?

There is wide agreement among scholars that the oldest and
most comprehensive description of Ageless Wisdom spirituality is
to be found in the Upanishads (part of the Vedic scriptures) of
India, which introduced the concept of Enlightenment to the
world. The Upanishads, the later texts of the Vedic scriptures,
possibly predated the Buddha and Vardhamana (also known as
Mahavira), the founder of Jainism, by about three to four centuries,
and gave rise to the form of spirituality we now know as "Hinduism."
"Hindu" is a term coined long ago by Muslims to refer to those
who lived on one side of the Sindhu river, which is south of modern
Delhi. Many Indians prefer to call their religion "Sanatana Dharma"
or the Eternal Teaching of the Law. Vivekananda, who presented
Hinduism to the world during the historic Parliament of World
Religions in 1893, explained:

> With the Hindus you will find one great idea:
> spirituality . . . The idea of unity, of the realization of God,
> the Omnipresent, is preached throughout. They think it is
> nonsense to say that God lives in heaven. That is a mere
> human, anthropomorphic idea. All the heaven that ever
> existed is here and now. One moment in infinite time is
> quite as good as any other moment. If you believe in a God,
> you can realize Him even now.

In Hinduism, the actual spiritual practice or path of
transcendence is called "yoga," which means a yoke or union. Yoga
connotes union with the divine as well as yoking oneself to
disciplined spiritual training. Yoga is divided into four basic paths,
which are suitable to different temperaments. The two central paths
are devotional love and wisdom, known respectively as Bhakti Yoga
and Jnana Yoga. The other two paths are Karma Yoga, selfless work
and service, and Raja Yoga, which is called the "scientific" path
because it treats the human self as a psychophysical experiment,
utilizing body, energy, and mind control techniques. The physical
yoga that is currently so popular in the West is Hatha Yoga, which
may be regarded as part of Raja Yoga. The ultimate aim of Raja

Yoga, however, is transcendence or Enlightenment and not merely keeping the physical body fit.

Inquiring into the reality of existence, which we have been discussing in this book, is the Path of Wisdom (Jnana yoga), which is similar to the Greek concept of *Gnosis* and *Sophia*. Buddhism is essentially a Wisdom path, but as we shall see, wisdom and love are connected. Although the early stages of the Wisdom path may involve just the intellectual study of metaphysical theory, the ultimate goal is to turn theory into practice—to realize and to actually live what started out as mere idea and theory. Knowledge in this sense is not just the collection of information but is intuitive and transformative. As in all mystic paths, this involves breaking the identification with the individual ego or "I" and coming to realize the reality of absolute Spirit or Atman in all—inside and out. Through contemplation, meditation, and metaphysical inquiry, we gradually strip away everything that is not the Real, cutting through the illusion of separateness and individual identity. The modern Indian sage Ramana Maharshi advocated the simple, profound, and unceasing asking of the question, "Who am I?" to break down our identification with the particular.

One of the simplest and most immediate practices recommended by the Buddha and other teachers over the ages is to pay dispassionate attention to the Here and Now, without any particular purpose or goal. Much of our lives is set on automatic pilot, propelled by the memories and experiences (our unquestioned "truth" or "reality") of the past and drawn forward by the future— desires, goals, dreams, fantasies, etc. Since the future is just a projection of the past, we are constantly driven by our conditioning factors, busy trying to get ahead and beat the "system" without ever really questioning the appropriateness of the system or our own actions. We have so much to do we rarely pay full attention to what is actually transpiring in the present moment. This cart-before-the-horse dynamic operates on us individually and collectively, resulting in much unnecessary waste, pain, and suffering.

If on the other hand we pay more attention to what is happening in the present moment, we will respond more aptly, directly, and spontaneously to the present, which is the only time we can really act. This response is not the result of conditioned, knee-jerk reaction or cumbersome analysis and reasoning but of "clear seeing" and "choiceless action." If we meet the challenge of the present adequately, the future will take care of itself.

Paying "bare attention" to the present opens up more inner spaciousness, which simultaneously helps us to avoid automatic reaction and increases self-knowledge, since we are able to see what drives us. Gurus or therapists cannot directly see and experience what is taking place within our consciousness. Only we can. In time, we will recognize that certain inner dynamics are common to all human beings. This will not only facilitate healing at the physical, emotional, and psychological levels, but open up new possibilities of being. The "I" will feel less solid and locked into specific perspectives and attitudes. It is important to remember that all of this arises by paying attention to "what is," without trying to get somewhere else or even wanting to make spiritual progress or attain enlightenment.

The Perennial Wisdom is not a shortcut to ecstasy or a way to avoid feeling emotional pain. We need to balance and integrate ourselves at whatever level or within whichever context is necessary (what Wilber terms "waves" and "streams"). If we come across pain, fear, or difficulty at work or at home, we must acknowledge it and, using it as a lesson, work through it and release it (i.e., not remained attached to it). This requires courage and resilience. Mystic teachers sought students not only with intelligence, but with mental and emotional stability, courage, and perseverance. Some Talmudic sages required that their students be married to try to ensure that they were in good sexual balance.

In his book, *Meditation in Action*, the well-known Tibetan Buddhist teacher, Chogyam Trungpa, pointed out that there are two basic types of meditation—that of the Heart (which will be discussed in the next section) and that of the Head or

Wisdom, which is concerned with the "discovery of the nature of existence":

> This basic form of meditation is concerned with trying to see what is . . . The achievement of this kind of meditation is not therefore the result of some long-term, arduous practise through which we build ourselves up into a "higher state," nor does it necessitate going into any kind on inner trance state. It is rather what one might call "working meditation" . . .

> The concept of nowness plays a very important part . . . One has to become aware of the present moment through such means as concentrating on the breathing . . . each respiration is unique, it is an expression of now . . .

> If one cultivates this intelligent, intuitive insight, then gradually, stage by stage, the real intuitive feeling develops and the imaginary or hallucinatory element is gradually clarified and eventually dies out . . .

> This is what one tries to achieve through Vipassana or "Insight" Meditation practice . . . Reality gradually expands so that we do not have a technique at all. And in this case one does not have to concentrate inwards but one can expand outwards more and more. And the more one expands, the closer one gets to the realization of centreless existence.

Alan Watts, in his *The Supreme Identity* written more than 50 years ago, also identifies two basic ways of realization—intense concentration, often directed to an external image of God and a second way which is very similar to Trungpa's description above:

> Far more suited to persons living in the world . . . it has its counterpart in the history of Western spirituality, (but) is especially characteristic of Chinese rather than Hindu tradition. While, like every spiritual exercise, it involves a

considerable degree of concentration and clear attention, it does not consist in removing all objects and impressions from consciousness save one. On the contrary, it is the ability to retain one's normal and everyday consciousness and at the same time let go of it. That is to say, one begins to take an objective view of the stream of thoughts, impressions, feelings and experiences which constantly flow through the mind. Instead of trying to control and interfere with it, one simply lets it flow as it pleases. But whereas consciousness normally lets itself be carried away by the flow, in this case the important thing is to watch the flow without being carried away. In the Chinese metaphysical tradition, this is termed wu-xin or "idealessness."

The Path of Devotion and the Heart

Comparing the Wisdom path of Jnana yoga with the more widely practiced Bhakti or devotional yoga, Professor Huston Smith writes in his best-selling *The World's Religions*:

> The yoga of knowledge is said to be the shortest path to divine realization. It is also the steepest, requiring a rare combination of rationality and spirituality . . . By and large, life is powered less by reason than by emotion and of the many emotions that crowd the human heart, the strongest is love . . . . The aim of Bhakti yoga is to direct toward god the love that lies at the base of every heart . . . . All the basic principles of Bhakti yoga are richly exemplified in Christianity.

Chogyam Trungpa writes of the devotional type of meditation:

> Where there is the concept of an external, "higher" Being, there is also an internal personality—which is known as "I" or the Ego . . . . This means that one feels oneself to be inferior and one is trying to contact something higher . . .

(This) is well known in the Hindu teachings, where emphasis is on going into the inward state of samadhi, into the depths of the heart. One finds a similar technique in the Orthodox teachings of Christianity, where prayer of the heart is used and concentration on the heart is emphasized. This is a means of identifying oneself with an external being and necessitates purifying oneself.

From the above excerpts and from the literature of various devotional traditions, we can deduce several characteristics of this approach. The most obvious is that it is driven by the emotions— togetherness, devotion, reverence, awe, ecstasy, and hopefully, unconditional love. Temples, churches, mosques, statues, paintings, artifacts, rituals, etc., are all designed to promote these feelings. Chanting, singing, swaying, and dancing are popular, and the larger and more enthusiastic the gathering of the faithful, the more powerfully the emotions are charged. It must be noted, however, that this kind of group dynamic is not restricted to religious gatherings but may be witnessed in political meetings, dance parties, rock and rap concerts, and tribal rituals.

The second characteristic is that since the spiritual seeker sees himself/herself as a devotee, worshipper, or lover, there has to be an Other, who is the object of devotion, worship, and love. Thus God is seen as "out there," separate from us and usually with specific, personalized attributes or qualities on which we can focus. If the aspirant does not go beyond this preliminary stage of Bhakti practice (which unfortunately is common), then God will forever remain separate and out of reach, a projection of our fears and desires that binds us tighter into our conditioning and our conflicts with others, who have different images of God. Devotees have fought and killed in the name of God throughout the recorded history of popular religion, and this phenomenon is still very strong in present times. It should not therefore be written off as unusual or unfortunate but acknowledged as an inherent part of the lower-level dynamics of the Devotional Path.

The dangers of an external god are increased if the aspirant is

convinced that she or he recognizes the one and only "God" or
God's special agent in the form of another human being. Putting
your will and your life in someone else's hands can and does lead
to abuse, and this is magnified in large groups where peer pressure
is added to the intoxicating mix. What we commonly call "cult
leaders" have been able to persuade their followers to commit even
mass murder or suicide for a variety of reasons—a passport to heaven,
purifying themselves, defeating evil, saving humanity, etc. The
dynamic that makes this possible is the same as that commonly
found in most churches and temples, except it is more extreme
and directed in a manner that society finds unacceptable.

The ultimate goal of Bhakti yoga is the same as Jnana yoga, which
is the dissolution of the sense of the separate self and union with the
divine. While the Jnana yogi does this by using discriminating wisdom
to continually strip away illusion, the Bhakti yogi progressively opens
to unconditional love and surrenders to the divine. The sixteenth-
century Christian mystic, Saint Teresa of Avila observed:

> In the spiritual marriage, the union is like what we have
> when rain falls from the sky into a river or fount; all is water.

The thirteenth-century Islamic Sufi teacher, Jelaluddin Rumi,
famous for his ecstatic poetry, often spoke of spirituality in terms
of love and separation from the beloved:

> Listen to the reed, how it tells a tale, complaining of
> separateness. Ever since I was parted from the reed-bed, my
> lament has caused men and women to moan. I want a bosom
> torn by severance, that I may unfold the power of love-
> desire: everyone who is left far from his source wishes back
> the time he was united with it . . . .

> The minute I heard my first love story, I started looking for
> you, not knowing how blind that was. Lovers don't finally
> meet somewhere. They're in each other all along.

Although devotional or heart spirituality is the most widely practiced because it is initially easier to feel inspired and elevated, final realization is not necessarily easy. Surrender must be complete and unconditional. We cannot bargain with the Absolute along the lines of, "I give you love and you give me what I want." In the final analysis, there really is no "Other" or separateness. Huston Smith, discussing Bhakti yoga as practiced in India, points out:

> Even village priests will frequently open their temple
> ceremonies with the following beloved invocation—
> O Lord, forgive three sins that are due to my human
> limitation:
> Thou art everywhere, but I worship you here;
> Thou art without form, but I worship you in these forms;
> Thou needest no praise, yet I offer you these prayers and
> salutations.
> Lord, forgive these three sins that are due to my human
> limitation.

Although the paths of the Head and Heart constitute the two fundamental paths to realization, they are not really separate. The Buddhists speak of the Twin Virtues of Wisdom and Compassion as being interrelated and necessary on the path to Enlightenment. In the Wisdom stream, stripping away the veils of illusion entails letting go of conventional attitudes and beliefs, of ego-defenses and eventually the sense of the separate "I." This necessitates opening the heart and surrendering. On the Devotional Path, surrender and devotion require the guiding light of wisdom or else we might spend our time creating and elaborating our own fantasy world or giving our lives over to deluded "masters," "gurus," or other impersonators of the Absolute. The following observations on Jnana and Bhakti yoga are from the modern sage Ramana Maharshi, whom Carl Jung described as "quite phenomenal. In India he is the whitest spot in a white space":

Surrender can take effect only when it is done with full
knowledge as to what real surrender means. Such knowledge
comes after enquiry and reflection and ends invariably in
self-surrender . . . .

The eternal, unbroken, natural State of abiding in the
(absolute) Self is Jnana. To abide in the Self, you must love
the Self. Since God is verily the Self, love of the Self is the
love of God; and that is Bhakti. Jnana and Bhakti are thus
one and the same.

The Path of Action and Work

The third spiritual path in the Hindu tradition is Karma Yoga—
action, work, and service in the everyday world. This path is for those
of an active nature. It recognizes that relatively few people can retire
to a cave or monastery in order to devote themselves exclusively to
their spiritual pursuits, and even solitude is not a guarantee of success.
It teaches that, with skilful practice, it is possible to find God in
everyday affairs and work, and this is most useful since it brings an
elevated consciousness to the other "quadrants" of life—culture, social
systems, etc. The approach to spiritual transcendence through work
was shared, among others, by the pragmatic Chinese and is particularly
suited to our modern, activity-oriented lifestyle where quiet and
seclusion are ever harder to find.

Karma yoga may be seen as the application of Bhakti and/or
Jnana yoga in daily life. The Karma yogi of the devotional bent
will dedicate her or his work to God rather than pursue selfish
personal motives that inflate the ego or sense of "I," an activity
that has been elevated as admirable in our present times. Each task
performed with a selfless attitude becomes an offering to God and
an execution of the will of God. In the West, Christianity, with its
emphasis on charitable works and good deeds, is a prime example
of this kind of Karma-Bhakti yoga. Mother Theresa was one of its
best-known modern practitioners. It should be noted, however,
that expecting praise and reward for your "charitable" works is not

letting go of ego but merely fortifying it in a less obvious way. All the positives and negatives that apply to the Bhakti yogi discussed in the previous section will obviously apply to the Kharma-Bhakti yogi, trying to live a spiritual life in the everyday working world.

For the Karma yogi who approaches work and action more from the perspective of Jnana yoga or discriminating wisdom, the concepts of "non-attachment" and "nowness" are important. What is done in each moment is appropriate (determined by heightened awareness and insight) to that moment without attachment to the result of that action. Surprisingly to many (because we have so few examples to witness), the result of such non-attached action is often much more effective than self-motivated action. In China and, subsequently, Japan, such an approach was very effectively used in martial arts, calligraphy, etc. Today, we can witness it in the truly exceptional athlete or artiste who can remain totally absorbed in the present moment. The Hindu classic, the Bhagavad Gita, advised:

> Perform thou right action; for action is superior to inaction, and inactive, even the maintenance of the body would not be possible . . . Action is duty, for by performing action without attachment, man verily reacheth the Supreme . . .

> All actions are wrought by the qualities of nature only. The self, deluded by egoism, thinketh, "I am the doer."

Vipassana meditation master Dhiravamsa writes in *The Way of Non-attachment*:

> The whole point of Buddhism may be summed up as living in the moment. It is also the point of life whether achieved through Buddhism, Christianity or any other religion. To live the truly religious life is to live fully from moment to moment, free from the past and the future. The past is the world of the dead because it has passed away. What is kept alive is only memories not facts. It is the past, which feeds disturbance and poison into the mind, preventing it from

being free, so that people do not open themselves to what is going on inside and outside them. The mind is occupied instead with its accumulated contents and individuals set up walls around themselves.

Emphasis on paying attention to the present moment is also found in the Chinese classic, *Dao De Jing*:

A thousand miles' journey begins from the spot under one's feet.
Therefore the Sage never attempts great things and thus he
     can achieve what is great.
He who makes easy promises will seldom keep his word.
He who regards many things as easy will find many difficulties.
Therefore the Sage regards things as difficult and
     consequently never has any difficulties.

Although the ultimate goal (achieved step by present step) of the mystic is transpersonal union with the Supreme, mystic training can give us extremely powerful tools for living in the everyday world. Karma yoga in particular teaches you about applying spirituality in the everyday world. In recent years, experts within the fields of psychology, corporate strategy, time management, stress reduction, etc., have begun to echo the above approach. The key to this approach, however, is non-attachment. This is not easy (especially if there are performance targets and bonuses or penalties), and the concept of non-attachment seems as yet little understood or implemented in the West. It is generally regarded as not dynamic and dramatic enough. It cannot be hoisted above your head in victory, worn like a designer suit, or driven ostentatiously down Main Street. It will not attract trophy husbands and wives like a magnet, although it is indeed an extremely valuable and rare quality.

The Esoteric Mind-Body Path

The fourth major spiritual path in the Hindu system is Raja or Royal Yoga. Some practitioners of Raja yoga claim that it includes all of India's yogic systems including Bhakti, Jhana, Karma, Mantra, Kundalini, Hatha, etc. It is also described by some as the Scientific Path because, as Huston Smith points out, it is "the way to god through psycho-physical experiments . . . unlike most experiments in the natural sciences, those of Raja yoga are on one's self." Raja yoga is systematic mind-body training aimed at self-transformation. The proof of this self-experiment is direct experience, to which no one else has access.

Swami Vivekananda writes of Raja yoga:

> Since the dawn of history various extraordinary phenomena have been recorded as happening amongst human beings . . . For thousands of years such phenomena have been studied, investigated, and generalized; the whole ground of the religious faculties of man has been analyzed; and the practical result is the science of Raja yoga. Raja yoga does not, after the unpardonable manner of some modern sciences, deny the existence of facts which are difficult to explain . . . There is no supernatural, but there are in nature gross manifestations and subtle manifestations. The subtle are the causes, the gross the effects.

The Raja yoga training includes eight basic steps: yamas (abstentions), niyamas (observances), asanas (posture), pranayama (control of breath), pratyahara (withdrawal of the senses), dharana (concentration), dhyana (meditation), and samadhi (contemplation or trance).

The first two steps of the Yamas and Niyamas cover the moral preliminaries that are found in all the other yogas and indeed in all major religious and spiritual traditions. The Judeo-Christian tradition has of course the Ten Commandments, and the Buddha's Noble Eightfold Path contains three foundational elements devoted to "Sila" or morality—Right Speech, Right Action, and Right Livelihood. In Raja yoga there are five restraints or abstentions—violence or injury, lying, stealing, sensuality, and greed. The five observances of self-discipline are cleanliness, contentment, self-control, self-study, and contemplation of the divine.

The control of body posture (asanas) and breathing would be familiar to all practitioners of Hatha yoga, which is excellent for health maintenance. Probably the most famous yoga posture is the cross-legged "lotus" position, which is used for meditation in many traditions because it brings such balance and stability to the body. Postures, however, may also include standing, lying, reclining, etc., depending on the specific purpose of the practitioner. The effect of these postures is enhanced by attention to detail, for which experienced teachers are most helpful.

In the West, the breath is generally regarded as something that just happens naturally . . . which indeed it does. But just as we can train and enhance the physical body (which also functions naturally), so we can learn to explore the function and potential of the breath. The science of breathing is known in Hinduism as "pranayama" and has a marked effect on the practitioner's "prana" or vital energy and indeed on the whole mind-body system. "Pranayama" literally means "control of prana." Different types of breathing can be used for general calming and stimulation as well as for more specific purposes relating to health and meditation practice.

The last four steps in Raja yoga are withdrawal of the senses, concentration, meditation, and contemplation. These constitute the various stages of what is generally known as "meditation." The first four steps are designed to slow down and quiet the body. The fifth step, withdrawal of the senses, is designed to turn the senses inward and prevent them from running after any stimulus that appears in consciousness. Psychologists estimate that the average mind cannot think of one thing exclusively for more than a few seconds at a time. No wonder the average person is skeptical of the enormous potential of the inner universe.

The sixth step in Raja yoga, concentration, is the development of one-pointedness or the ability to concentrate exclusively on one object, which may be either external or internal—a physical object, a sound (mantra), a color, the breath, the tip of the nose, the energetic centers (charkas), etc. Intensive concentration in this manner, especially on the charkas, may give rise to psychic phenomena and abilities.

In the seventh stage, meditation, the gap between subject and object begins to disappear. In the eighth stage of contemplation, the state of "samadhi" is attained, wherein there is union between subject and object, with the object's form and boundaries disappearing. Samadhi is recognized in other forms of Hinduism as well as in Buddhism. Ramana Maharshi advised:

> Samadhi alone can reveal the Truth. Thoughts cast a veil over reality and so it is not realized as such in states other than Samadhi. In Samadhi there is only the feeling of "I am" and no thoughts. The experience of "I am" is being still.

The Chinese mind-body system of "Qigong" bears several resemblances to Raja yoga. Qigong (sometimes spelled as "Chi Kung") literally means "skill in the matter of Qi or vital energy," which is also more or less the meaning of "pranayama". Like Raja yoga, Qigong features comprehensive training in the three main "regulations"— regulation of Posture, Breathing, and Mind. All these three aspects of being are seen as interrelated and inseparable from each other. Changes in any one aspect will affect the other two. Thus the body affects the emotions and mind; the emotions affect body and mind; the mind obviously affects both emotions and body. This applies in a negative way, as in disease and illness, and also in a positive way, as in moving to greater mind-body health and balance.

In Qigong, body postures are not only static—lying, sitting, standing, etc.—but also dynamic, including various kinds of walking as well as Taijiquan—like movements. These work in specific ways with the organs and meridians. "Mind" in this context includes the intellectual mind, the emotions and the "higher mind." "Mind regulation" consists of a wide variety of activities, including visualization of the Qi moving inside and outside the body, astral projection and objectless (empty) meditation, similar to that found in Buddhism and Hinduism.

The Chinese have traditionally applied Qigong in martial arts, health and healing and in spirituality. The concepts of Yin-yang and Qi are fundamental not only to Traditional Chinese Medicine but also to Chinese philosophy and culture generally. The Daoist "alchemists" sought to refine physical essence (*Jing*) into Qi and Qi into Spirit (*Shen*). In modern terms, this process can be interpreted as the transformation of consciousness although it is also an energetic process. The Shaolin Temple in Henan province, China is famous for its integrative mind-body practices. It gave rise both to the famous Shaolin Fighting Monks (who practiced Qigong) and to Zen Buddhism, which in China is called *Chan*.

This kind of mind-body or psychophysical training has not been historically common in the West although it has surfaced from time to time. The thirteenth-century Jewish mystic, Abraham Abulafia, who lived in Spain, apparently developed a yoga like system, which included concentration on the breathing, the repetition of mantras, and the practice of special postures.

In Summary

In Perennial Wisdom spirituality, the Divine is not only transcendent but also immanent. The spiritual destiny of the individual, therefore, is not merely to try to communicate with and obey God and his supposed Word, pending some distant Judgment Day, but to realize and become conscious of our own divine nature here and now. Carl Gustav Jung wrote of the Hindu master Sri Ramana:

> The identification of the Self with God will strike the European as shocking. It is a specifically oriental Realization, as expressed in Sri Ramana's utterances. Psychology cannot contribute anything further to it, except to remark that it lies far beyond its scope to propose such a thing. The goal of Eastern practices is the same as that of Western mysticism: the focus is shifted from the "I" to the Self, from Man to God. This means that the "I" disappears in the Self and Man in God.

The great eight-century Hindu Sage, Shankara, described union with the Absolute (Brahman) as follows:

> My mind fell like a hailstone into the vast expanse of Brahman's ocean. Touching one drop of it, I melted away and became one with Brahman . . . full of endless joy. How can I accept or reject anything? Is there anything apart or distinct from Brahman? Now, finally and clearly, I know that I am the atman (self), whose nature is eternal joy. I see nothing. I hear nothing. I know nothing that is separate from me.

To bridge the gap between the "I" and God, the Absolute, Spirit, etc., is not easy, but our present age seems to be calling for a profound shift in human consciousness. If we do not act in harmony with our true nature, which is Spirit itself, we will continue to cause conflict, confusion, and suffering on a rapidly expanding scale.

Following moral rules and thinking about philosophy and spirituality are admirable, necessary and helpful but insufficient to bridge this gap. Whenever the separate "I" manifests with its various types of conditioning and identification, there is always the "Other," separate in both space and time, and this separation causes us pain—conflict, frustration, anger, longing, grief, worry, fear, loss, etc. As an example, even though most people intellectually acknowledge that we need global cooperation to tackle the many problems that beset us, in practice we cannot get away from our "me first" mentality in our individual and collective lives, especially since society tells us we are being "unrealistic" for trying.

The intellect is capable of enormous imagination and creativity but is still limited by this duality and separation. Mystics throughout the ages have pointed out the limitations of the purely intellectual approach. The Greek saint, Gregory of Nyssa, explained, "Every concept grasped by the mind becomes an obstacle in the quest of those who search." The fourth-century Greek mystic, Evagrius Pontus, cautioned, "When you are praying, do not shape within yourself any image of the deity and do not let your mind be shaped by the impress of any form." "Approach the Immaterial in an immaterial manner." First-century Jewish theologian Philo Judaeus warned, "He who thinks that god has any quality and is not the One, injures not God, but himself."

The Ageless Wisdom tells us that there are two basic ways in which we may bridge this gap. The most popular path is that of devotion and love—Hindu Bhakti yoga, the Christian "sacred heart" of Jesus, the ecstatic love poems of the Islamic Sufis, etc. The love of God is the powerful, dramatic, emotional impetus that launches us on our spiritual quest. Eventually, however, the individual must move beyond asking for favors and completely surrender and dissolve in order to awaken to the realization that there is really no separate "I" or separate "Other," including God.

The other major path is that of the Head or Wisdom, which would include Jnana yoga and Buddhism. This approach consists of skillfully and persistently inquiring into life and especially oneself and stripping away whatever is false until all that remains is our essential Spirit shining forth and "enlightening" us. As with the path of the Heart, surrender is necessary and when we reach our final destination, there is no sense of separation.

We can apply this spirituality to everyday life as Karma yoga, Daoism, Chan Buddhism, etc. have suggested. Although we act without expectation of results and rewards, we are often surprisingly successful and efficient in what we do and may develop what appear to be extraordinary abilities. All of this requires that we turn our attention inwards and begin to explore the amazingly rich internal universe. The nineteenth-century Native American mystic Black Elk pointed out the power of stillness and silence—"Is not silence the very voice of the Great Spirit?"

In his book, *The Awakening of Intelligence,* Krishnamurti was asked by Swami Venkatesananda what he thought of the four main schools of yoga—Jnana, Bhakti, Raja, and Karma. The following is part of his reply:

> I have no authority—Sankara, Krishna, Patanjali, nobody—
> I am absolutely alone . . . First I want to find out how to be

free of this sorrow. Then being free, I shall find out if there is such a thing as God or whatever . . . I cannot sit by myself and dig into it because I may pervert it; my mind is too silly, prejudiced. So I have to find out in relationship with nature, with human beings . . . By being awake in relationship, I can spot it immediately . . . You watch while eating, when you are listening to people, when somebody says something that hurts you, flatters you. That means you have to be alert all the time . . . To watch, you need a very quiet mind. That is meditation . . . If you escape from the battle you have not understood the battle. The battle is you. How can you escape from yourself?

CHAPTER 5

AN AGELESS WISDOM VISION

There are numerous groups of expert, inspired, and dedicated people all over the world who recognize the need for fundamental changes in various aspects of our lives and are working on detailed blueprints for the future—environmental, scientific, political, economic, legal, medical etc. More often than not, however, these different groups are working to bring change only within their own specialized areas of concern because that is how our social systems are presently organized. There is still no broad coordination or common purpose between such groups and no popular, focused demand for change, with the result that the Establishment can easily deflect pressure for much-needed change, using the proven "divide and conquer" strategy. The average person may notice different groups calling for change and may be in agreement to a certain extent, but since no coherent alternative to the present system is presented, these calls just seem like more complexity, more decisions, and more stress. They are thus put aside.

I feel that Ageless Wisdom spirituality can be the common purpose and ground, from which we can launch ourselves into a future radically different from the bleak and soulless technological one that is presently being plotted for us. It can bring us the unity, joy, compassion, caring, fulfillment, purpose, and clarity of action, which are so conspicuously lacking in modern society. We live on a beautiful planet, which we are destroying through simple greed. Why do we not give priority to raising the real quality of our lives now rather than rushing ahead into a world of smaller, faster machines and genetic meddling, the implications and benefits of which are uncertain to say the least?

This chapter will explore a few of the possible ways that the knowledge and practice of Ageless Wisdom spirituality might spread and the effects this might have on us individually and collectively. It is one person's vision and hope, rather than a detailed plan or researched strategy. The details and plans will come once we have the will to change.

Finding a Voice

In a democratic society, it would seem that the first and most obvious step in increasing the awareness and practice of Ageless Wisdom spirituality is getting the message out where most people can be reached—primarily TV but also radio, newspapers, magazines, the Internet, etc.

In this endeavor, however, we immediately encounter three substantial obstacles. In the first place, the popular attention span has been progressively battered and attuned to mindless entertainment and titillation. We are accustomed to fifteen-second TV commercials that compete loudly for our attention and popular shows that feature increasingly titillating "eye candy" or some form of degradation or ridicule. On American TV, even broadcasters i.e. people who just talk, generally have to be attractive, especially the women. We change channels so fast, something (visual) must catch our attention within a second or two. Competing against this, ordinary-looking people speaking about spirituality and the generalized state of the world (without a current "hook" topic like immediate war or disaster) stand no chance. The standard advice is make the content quicker and slicker, but an alternative tactic would be to try to rehabilitate our attention span.

This "dumbing down" process is a vicious circle. Because the fast-paced, shocking, and titillating approach gets more attention and "works" in the short term, people from all walks of life (especially politicians) adopt it. The more they adopt it, the more "dumbing down" takes place and the easier it becomes to manipulate the audience since content is played down and entertainment tricks and effects elevated. This is yet another example of the gap between our technical ingenuity and our social ingenuity. Some thinkers feel that the technological is running faster than the personal development. I think a case can be made that in some ways, technological development is actually causing human beings to regress. In any case, there is definitely a gap.

As a current example of this trend, it is generally agreed that the administration of George W. Bush has used this approach more extremely and more effectively than any previous American administration. Out of the blue, certain simple phrases are repeated over and over again by various people, often accompanied by school-like banners bearing the same message, until the audience accepts that it must be true. Brazenly obvious (but seemingly effective) "photo ops" are arranged at the slightest hint of sinking popularity. Emotive and grand sounding phrases (usually exploiting American nationalism) are used even though they make no logical sense or may even be contradictory. No error is ever admitted and if contradictions, inaccuracies or falsehoods are proven, the approach is to talk about something else until people forget or get bored. In this respect, the "spinners" (of "truth") count on the fact that the audience's shortened attention span will prevent them from following the continuity and linkage of events. Sadly, this approach has proven effective for more than three years with no end in sight. Given the enormous economic and military power of the United States, such blatant manipulation is extremely alarming to the global population outside the U.S.A., many of who have easy access to CNN and can therefore witness it for themselves.

The second major difficulty in gaining media exposure for the Ageless Wisdom is that prime media time is very expensive, and someone has to foot the bill. In most cases, (corporate) sponsors are betting that viewers and readers will buy the products being hung on to the specific media content or at least retain their particular brand names in their memory banks, and this in the end will result in substantial net profits. To get the best value (i.e., number of viewers) for their sponsorship dollar, the safe and proven way is to cater to the popular taste, which as we have seen, tends to sink down to the lowest common denominator. The West sees itself as an advanced and sophisticated civilization, but if we step back and take an objective look at what is filling our prime time TV screens, it should give us pause for thought, as it does for example, the Muslim world. We tend to think of entertainment as innocuous fluff, but it exerts a powerful influence on our attitudes. We the ordinary people, on the basis of these haphazardly acquired attitudes, elect our leaders, who wield extraordinary and ever-growing power on our behalf.

Occasionally, prime media time is sponsored by a wealthy person or organization with whimsical, philanthropic, or "special interest" motives—i.e., someone has lots of money to spend on a pet project. This, however, is the exception rather than the rule and carries with it obvious, inherent dangers.

The third main obstacle that Ageless Wisdom exposure would likely encounter is that, all things being equal, media content has to obey the broad laws of political correctness. Crassness, crudity, humiliation, abusiveness, inanity, nudity, a wide variety of sexual acts, and explicit violence all apparently pass the politically correct acid test because they are examples of people "doing their own thing" and it makes us feel good that we are tolerant and sophisticated. The notion that levels of consciousness may vary from one person to another and that certain points of view may be qualitatively superior to others is a major postmodern taboo. We have discussed this subject earlier but I will repeat one point. The notion of a hierarchy of values is not the same as Nazism or fascism, because it includes and values all people within the human family. It actually gives us coherent reasons for explaining why Nazism and discrimination are unacceptable. If postmodernists condemn the Nazis, they break their own credo that all perspectives are equal. Is Nazism not a perspective?

At present, relatively little TV time is being given to

philosophy and religion, which is ironic given the global clashes between Islam, Judaism and Christianity and the radical scientific tampering with the genetic make up of biological species, including humans. What little is broadcast usually accords with the tenets of political correctness—let everyone do their own thing and tell their own inspirational story as long as they do not overtly criticize others. Interfaith discussions follow the same formula. Participants describe their own practices and beliefs but shy away from obviously contradictory and divisive issues like whether Muhammad was the final and thus most relevant Semitic prophet, whether Jesus was actually the only Son of God and if the Jews are the Chosen People, what happens to the rest. It is easy to see why these uncomfortable issues are avoided but if spiritual people cannot address (and maybe jettison) these beliefs, how can the ordinary people get past them? As a result, religious representatives tend to settle on moral platitudes like "we should all be more loving." The problem is that we are not particularly loving or tolerant despite centuries of this kind of religious exhortation. Because the beliefs of established religions are rarely challenged, we remain in massive denial, feigning aspirations to global unity but haunted by the crude, bloody, and recurring demons of centuries-old religious conflicts and power politics.

One of the most urgently needed and cost-effective investments that we as human beings can make is in a truly independent media organization—at least a TV station—dedicated to exploring the notion that there is a oneness underlying all human beings and there are forms of spirituality which reflect this. My feeling is that most people would be interested in—if not wildly enthusiastic about—knowledge that explains why we keep on killing each other in the name of God, love, and religion and the fact that there has long existed a more constructive, persuasive, healing, and unifying form of spirituality. Judging by results rather than verbiage, this type of work is not being done by existing organizations, including the major media, the main religions, the U.N., and certainly not individual countries. A representative of an organization usually represents the interests of that organization, which is not normally interpreted as dissolving that organization or giving up its power. An organization has a collective ego, and just like the individual ego, it does not normally want to give up power—at any cost. If we do not begin to let go of ego, however, wars will persist and be waged with ever more devastating weapons. Calling for world peace and harmony while beating a nationalistic drum is a logical contradiction, which for too long has been accepted as reasonable. It however allows us to pursue greed while thinking of ourselves as benevolent.

Even if I am completely wrong and absolutely no one is interested in inquiring into universal human nature and purpose, the financial cost of such a venture to a developed country or the U.N. would be like a proverbial drop in the bucket. How much does it cost to routinely operate a warship, submarine, or military aircraft, fire a cruise missile, put a man on the moon, or pay for the endless meetings (and pork barrel "consultants") at national parliaments, congresses, the U.N. etc., where the object is often to stall and obscure as much as possible, while furthering partisan agendas? How much does it cost to host a single meeting, with appropriate security and logistics, of the leaders of the rich G8 countries or a pope extravaganza? How much did it cost for George W. Bush to land on an aircraft carrier in the middle of the ocean with the world's media looking on, just to declare the Iraqi war over, when in fact it was not. Many millions of dollars of such expenditure routinely slip under the radar of public scrutiny. The financial downside of inquiring into ways of uniting humanity is minute compared to the possible rewards.

One of the main prerequisites of a media organization to inquire into the Ageless Wisdom would be the absence of any conditions attached to its funding except that it stays within its mandate and objectives (as stated above). This would immediately rule out advertising and the need to satisfy ratings quotients. Alternative sources of (obvious hands-off) financing could come from individuals and organizations—religious, philanthropic, or governmental, including the U.N. Such an initiative might focus both the interfaith movement and the U.N.—are we really aiming at unity and cooperation, or are we all content to keep playing the diplomatic, one-upmanship "pretend unity" game with the abundant cynicism of which certain countries openly boast? All this elaborate dance of deception costs a great deal of money as well as the goodwill of many ordinary people who clearly recognize the posturing and manipulation.

In such an endeavor, it would also be essential that those responsible for programming, research, and even the on-air personnel, be familiar with and accomplished in the Ageless Wisdom and be, without a shadow of a doubt, independent of existing organizations with vested interests, which would include established religions, lobby groups, political parties and countries. They must understand the difference between the Ageless Wisdom and popular religion and must be able to inquire beyond the smug declarations of belief and "truth" by religious representatives, which presently suffice as definitive answers.

As regards unity or universality, it seems that when we cut through all the specific theological ("belief in a supernatural, revealed god") and religious declarations and protestations, we finally come to a single basic question—are most of the main religions talking about the same basic god and moral code, or are we talking about totally different, irreconcilable gods and codes of conduct? If the former, then what is holding us back (apart from greed and power) from moving on to a more universal, harmonious, and healing spirituality? Extremely persuasive blueprints of such spirituality have been available to us for a long time, explaining in detail the obstacles to attainment.

Author Dr. Beatrice Bruteau, in her preface to Wayne Teasdale's *The Mystic Heart*, is optimistic about mysticism helping to bring about a fundamental spiritual shift:

> Nothing is more practical for realizing our desire for a better world than mysticism. Better worlds have to be built on sure foundations; they must be able to withstand deep impediments to their development. What most of us now recognize as a "better" world is one in which we recognize

that all people possess an incomparable value that we are all morally obliged to respect . . . But this view of moral obligation runs up against our inherited instincts of self-protection, greediness and desire to dominate others. We can try by various forms of legislation, to balance these two dynamisms, but they continue to conflict, causing tension and loss of energy. We are attempting to balance power from the outside. If we could rearrange energy from within—if we more often nurtured our companions and promoted their well-being, we would suffer much less. Rearranging energy from within is what mysticism does . . . The bell-wethers—the mystics—are gathering and uniting.

The Science of Self

What Dr. Bruteau described above as the ability to rearrange energy from within may be called the Science of the Subjective Self and is a field of study that is sorely neglected in contemporary society. We study everything around us, from atoms to constellations, and we even study the human brain (Wilber's upper right quadrant), but this is not the same as understanding what is taking place from a subjective perspective—from the inside (upper left quadrant) looking out. Without this subjective understanding and skill, it is not unusual to have our "buttons pushed" by certain people or events despite our best intentions and intellectual understanding.

If we are not aware whence or why our ideas, thoughts, instincts, emotions, wants, and needs arise, then we cannot logically know what we are doing in our individual lives is appropriate for ourselves—our habits, lifestyles, jobs, friendships, and intimate relationships. Collectively, this ignorance becomes far more dangerous when we attempt to rearrange the wider world with ever more fantastic schemes, making high-sounding but arrogant claims such as, "It is for the good of humanity." To understand "humanity," you must first understand yourself, and to understand yourself, you must inquire with great skill. If you only understand your own belief-driven religion within your own culture, the probabilities are that you are not very well qualified to speak for humanity. In our present area of specialization, few scientists and technologists are who striving to "improve" human life, have a broad, rounded education, much less expertise in the internal, spiritual arts and sciences.

Although the Buddha explained well over two thousand years ago why we are imprisoned by our own conditioning, most people today still tend to deny that they are in any way predictable or manipulated. Those same people, however, will unquestioningly accept the principle of "instilling values" at home, at school, and in the army and they may be employed in advertising, polling, marketing, sales, entertainment, media, teaching, or other attitude-shifting industries.

As a current example of this kind of "double-think", there is suddenly a strong demand for breast (and latterly chin, pectoral, penile and buttock) implants, cosmetic surgery and all kinds of face, hair and body alterations involving drugs, machinery, exercise equipment etc. Many of those buying into this trend deny that they are doing it because of fashion or to please others but for their own "self-esteem" or because it "makes sense." It should be obvious that notions of physical beauty are very much dependent on culture and society. If for example, you live by yourself on a desert island, it is unlikely to be a concern. If the adornments we undertake were just free, random choices, we would not all want the same look at the same time.

It is relatively easy to trace major components in the current beauty ideal. For men, it is largely traceable to (now Governor) Arnold Schwarzenegger in his debut movie, *Pumping Iron,* which turned bodybuilding from the ridiculous to the suddenly admirable. This trend in turn would not have been possible without the film industry, which subsequently made Schwarzenegger into an "action star," without the fashion and advertising industries jumping on the bandwagon, without the widespread use of steroids to produce unnaturally large and defined musculature, and without the added enthusiasm of the male homosexual community, which was also becoming fashionable in it own right.

For women, the current beauty ideal is a combination of the fashionable skinniness of 1960s models like Twiggy and the large breasts favored by the culture-shaping *Playboy Magazine*, which also rose to prominence in the 1960s. Since this level of skinniness rarely occurs naturally and especially not in conjunction with large breasts, nature needed considerable help. Thus arose eating disorders, drugs, exercise mania, and cosmetic surgery, each becoming enormously profitable industries in their own right. The media has been politically correct, careful about endorsing cosmetic surgery outright, but giving it a lot of exposure on the grounds of education, celebrity gossip and positive "make-over" stories, replete with cheering friends and family. Some even go so far as to tout cosmetic surgery as a form of political or spiritual liberation! A survey conducted by *Psychology Today* magazine found that women were rapidly becoming dissatisfied with their bodies—25 percent in 1973, 38 percent in 1986, and 56 percent by 1997. This seems at odds with a more enlightened attitude, especially since the number of women in positions of power within the media, fashion and entertainment industries has been steadily growing. The enthusiasm for this kind of "improvement" also gives an added impetus to those now researching genetic and robotic modification and implants.

Although religious people tend to think of themselves as concerned with the "inner" world (shunning for example, obsession with physical beauty), more often than not, their lives also depend on trying to arrange the external world. God, in his role as Creator, Rule-maker, Judge etc., is generally seen as outside of ourselves and needs to be placated. The church or temple, with its organizations, rules, inspirational gatherings, and donation drives, is also a powerful external influence. The masses of both believers and non-believers are outside. Considerable importance is given to (externally verifiable) ritual behavior within holy places and "moral" behavior (as defined by the believers) in general life. Followers of popular religion have over the centuries consistently killed in the name of their religion and god and continue to do so because matters in the "external" world do not accord with their views.

In the climate we have created wherein time is money, understanding yourself is regarded as a waste of time because it does not result in a direct monetary or social reward. The well-balanced and helpful citizen becomes invisible to modern society. You are much more highly rewarded if you can persuade and manipulate others, regardless of the intrinsic value of what you are advocating. Even screwing up your life can bring rewards and visibility within society because you can then "recover" and sell the story of your brave and inspiring recovery.

The journey into the Self must be open ended and cannot be conditional upon rewards or "results," yet that does not mean that one's life cannot change radically for the better or that the impact of such change on society is negligible. On the contrary, such change ripples out into every aspect of one's being and into the wider world.

It is difficult to describe the specific changes that Ageless Wisdom spirituality would have on an individual since each journey is unique and the aim is to open and flow with life rather than conform to a specific way of acting—being "holy" or "pious". There are no obvious, foolproof rules or signs (apart from perhaps analyzing the minutiae of brain patterns, biochemistry, etc.) that mark the evolution of consciousness. The smiling, gentle, all-knowing archetype of the saint or guru is attractive and not inaccurate, although there have been many examples of volatile and irascible spiritual teachers. In addition, the above spiritual archetype is easily mimicked and exploited by charlatans and "marketers." The journey from our present state of consciousness to complete Enlightenment is likely a long one. It is far more important that we get started in the right direction, than to quibble about what it would be like being there.

For the sake of simplicity and specificity, I will offer hereunder some brief observations based on my own experiences as an individual on the Path and as a teacher and healer. I can unhesitatingly attest to profound changes in my own life but, in so doing, make no claim of supreme attainment. This is just a snippet of my own story.

A Personal Journey

My first experience of self-transformation came when I was between eight to ten years old living in Guyana, the country of my birth. As a child, I had an extremely explosive temper, which kept getting me into more serious trouble the older I got. I curbed my temper by repeating to myself hundreds of times, "I must not get angry" until my anger indeed subsided. Around that same period, I became afraid of an especially fierce teacher, who had caned me (repeatedly hit on the hands and buttocks with a cane) on several occasions. I created a new phrase to repeat to myself. "He is only a human being, just like me." After a while, my fear also went away. No one had counseled me because I somehow felt I had to deal with it myself. At that time, no one I knew had heard of mantras or affirmations.

People have come to the realization (or at least the possibility) of Deep Spirituality in a variety of ways—death, loss, illness, love, a knock on the head, the glimpse of a flower, etc. I came to it when I first read about Buddhism. At that time, I was attending the London School of Economics (LSE), which was one of the centers of the Student Revolution in Europe. Although I was very enthusiastic about Christianity throughout my time at primary school, by my university days I had come to regard religion in Marxian terms as "the opium of the people." I was interested in and formally studying philosophy, politics and economics, but I had not discovered anything that seemed to provide all the answers I needed. Every system historically seemed to fall into an action-reaction, thesis-antithesis, us-them dynamic.

I picked up Christmas Humphreys' book *Buddhism*, because Zen was becoming trendy and I felt I needed some background in order to debunk it properly. To my great surprise, however, the Buddha's teachings explained life, particularly human behavior, in a way that was far more consistent and complete than any other philosophy, science, or religion I had encountered. It was like a light bulb suddenly turning on and illuminating the surrounding darkness—many things came into plain view and their relationships became obvious. I realized for the first time how the thinking mind was limited and why at times it would be appropriate for it to be silent.

The Buddha stated that everything (including our sense of self and our thinking process) is continually changing and conditioned by a multitude of factors, which are in turn changing and conditioned. He said that we suffer because we persist in trying to do what is impossible—make life solid and fixed; grasp and keep the "good" bits while we push away or avoid the "bad." In reality, good and bad are interrelated and in a state of flux. We ourselves are in a state of flux and on a (largely denied) journey towards eventual decay and death. I could clearly see these processes, including all the accompanying emotions of greed, worry, fear, envy, anger, sadness, etc., operating within myself at many different levels. When I looked more closely at other people, I could discern the same universal dynamics beneath the surface. The Buddha suggested that the answer to our problems was simply to let go of attachment. That was the one form of "action" that never ever entered my mind! I had hitherto sought more control, not less.

With almost childlike enthusiasm and fascination, I started observing my internal patterns through formal periods of quiet, sitting meditation and in the course of my daily life. I was startled at how many processes were taking place beneath the level of my usual awareness and how little real control I had over my life. My mind was always busy, often veering off in a seemingly random manner. Many of these observations corroborated what the Buddha taught and so I expanded my reading not only about Buddhism, but about religion, spirituality and occultism.

As I continued with my daily meditation practice, my mental activities slowed and would sometimes stop, almost as if they did not like being observed. This process was reflected in my external demeanor, which slowed down, relaxed and became more centered. I noticed more internal spaciousness, which simultaneously prevented me from falling into knee-jerk reactions and enabled me to see the wider and deeper connections between my various behavioral and thought patterns. Much of what previously had seemed random was not. There was a dramatic reduction in my need to judge and control other people and in worry, guilt, conflict, projection, identification, possessiveness, frustration, anger, etc. This in turn freed up more energy and zest for life, which steadily became clearer and simpler as I learned to take life one day and one moment at a time. I applied this in my martial arts (judo and karate) training, which I had taken up the year before. Martial arts in turn helped my discipline, focus and my overall health.

One of my first big challenges in applying Buddhism to everyday life occurred in the early stages of my chartered accountancy training. I undertook the training after university because it was "safe and sensible," my father wanted me to do it, and I could not think of what else to do. It was a guaranteed source of good income and would give me a broad-based understanding of the business world and our economic and financial systems. Once started, however, I found the actual work extremely tedious, the surroundings sterile, and many of my "superiors" arrogant and small minded. I wasted as much time as I could around the water cooler and counted each minute to the end of the day and to the weekends. I was in deep conflict, torn and divided. Like so many other people, I hated my work.

After a few months of this, it suddenly occurred to me to try to apply the Buddha's teachings, and so I set out in meditation to determine "clear comprehension of purpose." Within a short time, it became clear that although the training was not intrinsically fulfilling or exciting, the "right action" in my circumstances was to finish the training I had undertaken. With my newfound clarity, I applied myself wholeheartedly to my work and studies. In the spirit of Karma yoga, I took pride in doing each task to the best of my ability and letting the results take care of themselves. I stopped carrying work concerns home with me; time seemed to move much faster. That simple internal adjustment immediately and completely transformed my working life and this in turn rippled out into the rest of my being. It was my first major test in applying the Buddha's teachings to a "real" life problem, and I was amazed at the extent of my success.

During my accountancy training and practice, I did mostly "auditing" jobs, which necessitated working for extended periods at the premises of different businesses. I interviewed people from all levels of each business from CEOs to the most menial worker. I worked in boardrooms, offices, factories, hotels, warehouses, farms, docks, etc. This proved to be an invaluable opportunity to observe and interact with people from all walks of life. Since I was an impartial outsider, they would often treat me as a sort of therapist and share with me their innermost thoughts, feelings, disappointments, dreams, and plans for retirement. Beneath the common façade of contentment and normality, there was much suffering and confusion. If they sought advice, I would try to explain the Buddhist perspective and it often proved helpful.

In 1974, several events came together to intensify and deepen my Buddhist and martial arts practices and indeed my life. I decided to make a commitment to the practice of Buddhism and in particular to Vipassana (Insight) meditation. Through the Buddhist Society, I met and started studying with Thai meditation master, V.R. Dhiravamsa. After years of searching for genuine masters of the Chinese martial arts, I found Shaolin master Tan Choo-seng in Singapore and "internal" arts master, Rose Li, in London.

I choose Dhiravamsa because, although he was a traditionally trained monk, he used practices from western psychotherapy and other spiritual traditions to help students break through their barriers, including the emotional ones. I did not find it too difficult to sit quietly in meditation but I found emotions messy and kept tight control of them and of all my relationships. Although I felt fear in opening up to emotional exploration, I knew I could not sidestep it if I was serious in my spiritual practice. My retreats with Dhiravamsa were extremely intense, giving me the feeling that I was living through years of life in actual weeks or months. As I did this, my heart opened more and more until I could let go and surrender. I could truly love . . . without conditions or control. I proposed marriage to my girlfriend, Yolind.

I found that as I progressively let go of my defensive and controlling mechanisms, my world did not fall into chaos, and I could simultaneously sense and feel more. As the tyrannical and incessant voice of the intellect began to subside, I became more acutely aware that the other parts of my being each had its own intelligence and voice. The physical and primal body spoke to me as did the emotional Heart, which sought relationship and connection with others. As I took one step at a time, every day and every moment was excitingly brand-new rather than jaded and boring. A minute ago, no matter how painful, frustrating, or insensitive, was a minute ago; this is now and an opportunity to start afresh!

Over time, I developed a detailed knowledge of my own internal world—not only of mental and emotional patterns but how these interacted with the physical body in the area we call "health." The more I learned about myself, the more I learned about others since we share many common mind-body mechanisms—just as under our very different physical appearances, the bones, organs, blood, etc., look and function very much alike. Later on in life, I discovered that various formal systems like Traditional Chinese Medicine, Qigong, the Chinese "internal" martial arts, and the Enneagram personality types (used by the Sufis), also included as part of their teaching several of the processes I had observed for myself through the Vipassana practice of "bare attention."

At the age of thirty-four, I accepted Dhiravamsa's offer to train as a teacher of Vipassana, leaving my job as an accountant. I never returned to it, instead embarking on an uncertain, self-created career path as a teacher of Vipassana and Taijiquan in Toronto. I made this decision just after the birth of our second daughter, Shu-wei. My wife Yolind was outwardly supportive but the prolonged financial insecurity was among the factors that caused her to ask for a separation and divorce in 1993, about nine years after my career change.

As I look back on that fateful decision, I have no regrets and no sense of pain although if I think of it, there were times that might be construed as difficult. Yolind's separation demand was a shock not only to me, but also our children. Although it was a difficult period, I think we all came out of it well, thanks in no small part to meditating together, being able to share our feelings and spending much time together, which was one of the positives of my kind of work. The marital breakup sparked an exodus of some of my teachers, who had been training intensively with me for several years. It was a disturbing loss because they represented a very small elite of our organization's students, the vast majority of who come, dabble a bit and then leave. It was also disheartening because the reasons for their leaving arose from personality, unresolved emotional issues, and postmodernism, all of which we had discussed and worked on well before the breakup. I felt very alone at that time and questioned myself deeply, but could see nothing else I could have done that would have made more sense. I continued on my teaching path, taking one step at a time. Most of the teachers who stayed are still with me.

At this point in time, I love and appreciate life and indeed always have, ever since I understood Buddhism. Although my teaching has not made me rich in a monetary sense, it made me rich in relationships, unexpected experiences, love, knowledge and life. My three daughters are beautiful and loving people. I have found love after Yolind. I have represented my country as a performer and judge in the Chinese martial arts, as have some of my senior students. I have had the opportunity to meet with and learn from talented fellow teachers and through one, Dr. Jerry Alan Johnson, studied Traditional Chinese Medicine and Medical Qigong Therapy, becoming a qigong healer nearing the age of fifty. I have had one book published (*The Conscious I*) and have two more (including this one) in the works. I have just designed and built (at times, physically) an off-grid retreat center that incorporates both the latest sustainable energy technology and the age-old wisdom of *fengshui*.

As I go through life, I continually surprise myself by learning new skills and acquiring new knowledge. All of this, however, only serves to fill in the details of the broad outlines that I discovered so many years ago and keeps on confirming for me, the underlying oneness of all humanity.

One of the greatest gifts I have received in my life is the ability to love and be loved. I could not (and did not, before Buddhism) truly love without consciously accepting the real possibility of pain, including conflict, loss, betrayal, etc. Love is. It has no conditions. It requires an open heart. I point this out because in our present marketing climate, wherein language is being ever devalued, we attach the word "love" to so many things it has become somewhat meaningless and confusing. Love is not power, obligation, co-dependence, reward, jealousy, sex, security, "trophy" partners, etc. It is certainly our right to choose such relationships, but when we attach the word "love" to them, we lose sight of something precious, which is actually our birthright.

Morality and Law

During the rest of this chapter, we will consider how aspects of our collective lives might be affected by a general transformation of consciousness within individuals to the highest "personal" level. As we have seen in chapter three, this level, though still far short of complete enlightenment, will increase our understanding of our individual "self," will enable us to discern subtle cause and effect and make us actually (not just ideally) capable of a global, multicultural perspective.

Even an elementary understanding and practice of the Ageless Wisdom would lead to a higher and more consistent standard of morality since "doing good" would come from direct insight into oneself and life rather than pressure to conform to an external, often arbitrary standard or expectation. In the latter case, there is always a way to get around the strict letter of the law in order to further one's self interest. In addition, individuals have long felt and are now increasingly saying it aloud, "Why should I not put myself first when our leaders and respected institutions do it all the time?" "If our country can kick ass when riled, why can't I?" Those are actually valid and relevant questions.

As soon as we begin to look into ourselves and discover the subtle dynamics there, we will begin to recognize them in other people and even in nature. Furthermore, we will see interconnections and sequences of cause and effect that previously escaped our attention. We will realize that in our universe it is impossible to get "something for nothing," that much of our discontent arises from our own internal causes, and that because of our innate interconnectedness, when we hurt or exploit others, we also hurt the larger community and ourselves. All of this will result not from trying to follow laws and teachings, but because we see it directly and unequivocally. It therefore becomes "natural," "obvious," and "common sense."

This higher subjective quality of judgment and morality will dramatically lessen conflict and simplify our lives. When we learn how to recognize and resolve our individual and family problems early on, they will not grow into issues that involve the various social services, police, courts, and legislature. On the international level, the use of coercion, armies and fantastic weapons systems will diminish. This would save an enormous amount of expenditure, simplify life (less regulation and red tape), and free up resources for more deserving and urgent matters.

Much of the conflict stemming from promoting and defending our (self) identity—gender, sexual, national, racial, religious, political, professional, etc.—will simply evaporate. There is in fact nothing sacred about identity. It is conditioned and changeable like everything else. It can certainly lift us up, but it can also bring us down, sometimes to disaster. When we are able to see ourselves and our world in terms of "both-and" rather than "either-or," there will be no need to fight over identity. We will still be able to appreciate our traditions, history, differences, and individuality but at the same time acknowledge our greater humanity.

Playing on identity is one of the main strategies used by those who seek to manipulate and divide us, whether extremists, politicians, marketers or hustlers. It is primitive and crude but at the moment, still very effective, because we allow it to be so. We abhor this trait when we see it in other nations but nevertheless feel it is appropriate for our own nation. Even before September 11, politicians knew it was a failsafe ploy to end big speeches and statements with, "God Bless America." If God is indeed the creator not only of this planet but of the entire universe, however, why would we think he (or she) would want to bless just America? Moreover, in this age of the so-called global village, why would we even ask?

Our social institutions will obviously need to adjust to this new level of consciousness. Within the legal system, for example, a more sophisticated understanding of complex cause and effect will raise the bar of responsibility and accountability and necessitate better rules of evidence. At present, the courts understandably reflect the confusion and inconsistency of most individuals. There are ongoing arguments about whether individual action is determined by internal or external circumstances and whether or not past actions are indicative of present conduct. In both these matters, the truth is "both-and" rather than "either-or." In terms of the impact of past actions, a double standard is often applied. Jurors are presumed to be impartial, yet can be routinely challenged and even excluded on account of their general past actions. At the same time, a wide range of past actions of the accused are commonly excluded from evidence. Much of this kind of confusion arises from the inability of postmodernism to recognize qualitative distinctions.

A better understanding of human dynamics will lessen the inappropriate application of "precedent" and the manipulation of the jury (and judges) by physical attractiveness, dress and mannerisms, all of which send subtle (and often not so subtle) social signals. It will also allow juries to better evaluate "experts," who often boast dubious qualifications and are up for sale to the highest bidder.

Recognizing more subtle and complex cause and effect will also raise the level of accountability in the "external" world in such matters as the environment, advertising, corruption, fraud, etc. This will be strongly contested, however, because of the traditionally narrow definition of cause and effect within western legal systems and the enormous legal war chests of the corporations, which have a vested interest in maintaining the present legal smoke screens. Talking of which, consider how long it took for the legal and judicial systems to recognize that cigarettes damage your health. Apologists for the tobacco industry acted outraged at the mere suggestion that a harmless practice like holding the smoke from ignited chemicals within your lungs over a period of years could possibly be a health hazard! Not only is this kind of stance grotesque, but also the fact that we as a society have given it credence for so long.

Other specific changes to the current legal and justice systems are needed. Firstly, it is far too easy for money to tilt the scales of justice. A corporation or individual who can pay high-priced lawyers indefinitely can simply outspend (and even bankrupt) an opponent. Secondly, we should reconsider the logic that defense lawyers, who know their clients are guilty, are somehow serving the cause of justice by shielding them from liability.

Thirdly, it is unrealistic to expect ordinary, untrained citizens (and even most judges) to coherently sort out complex issues of psychology much less matters like stem cell research, cloning, robotic, and nano-technological implants, etc. Much of this turns on understanding who we are at a profound level (including our identity as Spirit), and that is currently not part of our education. Many of the conclusions and attitudes of the average citizen are simply wrong headed and while that may be democracy, it can also lead to disaster in age where technology is not only incredibly powerful but also evolving much faster than humans can even fully comprehend, much less use with restraint and wisdom.

I do not think that general consciousness will evolve fast enough to cope with the many technology-generated issues, which will soon need consideration within the legal system. Perhaps we can replace the system of a single judge or judge and jury with a panel of three judges, representing not only narrow scientific and technological expertise but the broad well-being of human beings as well as the planet itself.

In this latter category, I would suggest a representative of the Ageless Wisdom tradition be a part of such panels since its basis is the oneness of all humanity, the recognition of subtle cause and effect and expertise in human consciousness and internal functioning. The Ageless Wisdom does not advocate or facilitate discrimination, exploitation, projection, denial, deceit, building power bases, etc. For those who are concerned about elitism and civil liberties, we can reform the appeals system and perhaps add a review system to keep a check on these new judge panels.

Environment, Economics, Science, and Politics

The individual who is capable of a global perspective, integrative "both-and" thinking and recognizing complex, multi-level cause and effect will make consumer, lifestyle, and political decisions, which will be very different from today's norm. Such decisions in turn will roll out into all quadrants of our lives, impacting our culture, social systems, research etc.

The realization that our personal destiny and quality of life is in a very real sense linked with all beings on this planet will radically shift all our thinking. We will no longer find it reasonable to justify plundering and poisoning the planet by expecting science to come up with a miracle or hoping it will just go away. We will reconsider the logic of bettering society by making the relatively small number of rich even richer even as millions starve. We will rethink the strategy of making the world safer by making ever more devastating weapons faster than other countries. It will begin to dawn on us that as robots and computers keep doing more and more work, there is less work for humans and that unless we share the profits of this productivity and reduce dependence on robots, more humans will be reduced to menial tasks or will become superfluous. We will finally demand a satisfactory answer to the question why we continually kill in the name of a loving god. We will begin to inquire into why our championship of equality consistently results in more inequality (with ourselves coming out on top).

We do not all have to become self-denying saints . . . just start making smarter and more compassionate decisions. The most immediate and effective are our buying decisions. Right now, we can demand motor vehicles that last longer, are more fuel efficient and less toxic, although we may have to give up our infatuation with minor annual "sexy" alterations to the shape and color of cars. This simple adjustment will boost our personal finances through cost and maintenance savings while greatly reducing environmental pollution and destruction. We can demand food with less fat, oil, salt, sugar, preservatives, additives, and processing, including genetic modification. We can also simply eat less. Over the past few years, the food industry, quite aware of the explosion of obesity in North America, has nevertheless been increasing the size of food portions. We can stop or at least consider the consequences of buying our kids video games, especially those that feature killing and violence. One consequence of this is that parents may have to spend more time with their children, which presumably would have been one of the reasons for having children in the first place. We can demand less packaging and recycle what there is. When it is hot we can sweat (which is healthy); when it is cold, we can put on more clothes. We do not have to control the temperature of a whole house or building in order to regulate our individual body temperature. Office workers wearing sweaters on a sizzling hot summer's day or flimsy shirts in the middle of winter is not only a sign of tremendous energy waste but may also be damaging to health, according to various traditional forms of medicine. None of the above measures requires money or advanced technology to implement.

Come election time, we can vote for representatives who are experienced, honest, caring, and intelligent rather than those who just look good, are smooth talkers, or perhaps famous. Much of this can be achieved by simply paying attention to what would-be vote getters say over a period of time. We can generally support politicians who want to "level the playing field" by limiting campaign contributions and curtailing influence pedaling by those in power. In America, for example, it has become so common for politicians to shuffle between big corporations and government that the average person seems not to care about the far-reaching implications of such practices. Probably the highest profile such case currently is that of Vice-President Dick Cheney. In 1995, he became the CEO of Halliburton, a Dallas-based multibillion-dollar oil services company and defense contractor. His main qualification for such a job seems to have been the fact that he served under three (now four) presidents, including secretary of defense under George Bush Sr. During the five years Cheney was CEO, Halliburton doubled its business with the American government to $2.3 billion at the same time as it doubled its political contributions to $1.2 million, overwhelmingly to Republican candidates. Cheney continued to be paid substantial "deferred compensation" by Halliburton even when serving as vice-president and to hold Halliburton stock options. When victory was declared in Iraq, a Halliburton subsidiary was awarded the first big rebuilding contracts, estimated to be worth over $1 billion. There have been reports that Halliburton, under Cheney (known for his anti-Iraqi stance,) traded with Libya, Iran, and Iraq and used "aggressive accounting" to book speculative rather than actual profit, thereby helping to raise Halliburton's share prices.

It must be noted that in the post-Reagan Free Market era, large corporations benefit not only from overt tax breaks but also from giant government contracts and lax regulations, all of which act as unmonitored transfers of wealth from the poor to the rich. While a handful of companies like Halliburton get the lucrative contracts, the average taxpayer foots the bill for the war, its "collateral damage," subsequent policing operations, etc., which in the case of Iraq, will mean hundreds of billions of dollars added to the national deficit. The same mechanism operates when a big company is allowed to avoid the social costs (like health and environmental damage) of its actions, while the taxpayer pays for the emergency cleanups, hospital bills, etc. American embassies and other government departments routinely lobby and sometimes provide credit to get overseas business for American companies, including Halliburton. Yet again, all these expenses are paid by the ordinary taxpayer.

Large governments spend by the billions, and when all is said and done, a relatively small number of people control spending. Whenever there is money to be made, those whose primary interest is money will be attracted, and there will be corruption . . . Take money out of the equation, and most of these people will disappear. Such changes can only strengthen democracy, but no doubt the entrenched powers will find some reasons to object because they presently enjoy a most lucrative arrangement. As regards the small number of people who control spending and the supposed division of powers, it is interesting to peruse the social pages of newspapers and magazines and see the same faces time and time again at the most influential gatherings.

Society has changed so rapidly, perhaps it is time to overhaul the two-party systems in countries such as America, Canada, and the U.K. It is ludicrous and very cumbersome to think that every issue should arbitrarily fall into an "either—or" category of Liberal/ Democratic/ Left on the one hand and Conservative/ Republican/ Right on the other. As we have seen, the archetypal Republican and Democratic perspectives represent two different levels of consciousness. In turn, the highest level of personal consciousness transcends both. On a practical note, most of these parties have been around so long, they are part of the system of government and as such wield an enormous amount of power, whether or not they have been elected. This is not good for democracy because it makes it difficult (almost impossible) for smaller parties and fresh, constructive ideas to make an impact.

The present party systems, especially in America, are biased towards personality politics to the detriment of specific issues. In the first place, it takes a lot of money to run for high office, so a successful candidate must either be fabulously wealthy or be able to muster financial backers, who will eventually want favors in return. In addition, since voters are essentially buying a vague party package of policies rather than voting on single issues, voters tend to pick the candidate they like best—usually as seen and heard on TV. As we have seen, celebrity has become a desirable and mesmerizing quality in itself. All of this would tend to suggest that actors or natural performers would make successful candidates, and this is indeed proving so—Reagan, Clinton, and George W. Bush, and in England, Tony Blair, another actor. Intelligence, experience, and honesty are not enough or may not even be necessary. Arnold Schwarzenegger got elected as Governor of California almost totally on his personal finances, his political connections and his celebrity, since he steadfastly kept interviews and policy statements to an absolute minimum. Voters thought they "knew" him on the basis of his films and media appearances and that was more than enough.

The need for reelection every few years gives voters some leverage, but it also creates a bias towards popular short-term policies with the consequent neglect of vital long-term projects like the environment, etc. It has also become common for departing politicians to pay off their friends with patronage and to push through damaging policies, the true costs of which do not become evident until some time after the politicians have left office and are safely retired or ensconced in some corporate ivory tower.

A possible remedy might be to use the Senate or House of Lords as an impartial, advisory, appointed (non-elected) body, similar to a traditional council of wise elders. At present, such appointments (in the U.K. and Canada) are mainly used as political rewards by the government of the day. Perhaps criteria for selection to this revamped body might include expertise in specific areas (science, spirituality, ecology, etc.) as well as the absence of affiliation to specific political parties. Appointees could be given special training to acquaint themselves with the fundamental issues of humanity, including developing technologies as well as the Ageless Wisdom. Their job would be to pinpoint issues crucial to society and to give general, longer-term guidance to society—issuing recommendations and perhaps selecting issues for legislation or referendum. Referendum issues could include a special long-term category, covering issues like the environment, cloning, genetics, and robotics, which would require more than a simple 51 percent majority to alter—perhaps at least 70 percent.

Rules and laws can also be implemented to make our political and bureaucratic rulers subject to similar financial, legal, and ethical standards as ordinary citizens. Many in government see themselves as CEOs and officers of national corporations and have been pushing for salaries, compensation packages, and pensions similar to the private sector, so why should they be excused from the responsibilities and liabilities that go with such jobs? It seems that those in power should be subject to higher not lower standards of responsibility than individuals, especially since the taxpayers also pay their legal bills. For example, someone in government who is responsible for or connected with awarding government contracts should not, on leaving government, be allowed to receive payments from companies who have benefited from such contracts, since this would amount to "deferred compensation." Similarly, if someone in government has been negligent or criminal, they should be held responsible. An error or ignorance of the law does not necessarily protect an individual citizen.

Perhaps, there is a movement in this direction. In December 2003, the Supreme Court of Canada unanimously (9-0) ruled that public officials can be sued for the harm they cause by deliberately failing to perform their public duties. This failure referred to "bad faith", rather than mere inadvertence or as a result of budgetary constraints. The particular case concerned the refusal of up to twenty police officers, who witnessed a shooting by a colleague to cooperate with an investigation into it.

The effects of an advance in individual and collective consciousness obviously would not be restricted within the borders of individual countries. Ervin Laszlo, in his book, *Macroshift: Navigating the Transformation to a Sustainable World*, writes about possible political changes:

> Lifting the sights of national politicians above the borders of their countries and focusing them on regional and global economic, political, social and ecological issues is an urgent step whose time has come. The sovereign nation-state is a historical phenomenon: it appeared on the world scene only at the 1648 Peace of Westphalia . . . Decision-making in a world dominated by nation-states is cumbersome, as seen in

the experience of the United Nations. Yet there is nothing in the psychology of citizenship that would forbid the expansion of people's loyalty above the level of the nation state . . . A downward transfer of the sovereign powers of national governments is urgent in regard to education, employment, social security, social and economic justice and local resource use. But an upward transfer is necessary as well in regard to peace and territorial and environmental security.

I was pleasantly surprised to read, some time ago, an article in the *Globe and Mail* newspaper by John Gray, on Paul Martin, who became Canada's Prime Minister in December, 2003. In the article, excerpts of which are included below, Martin spoke about the need for more global cooperation. Admittedly words are cheaper than action, but I was encouraged that they were spoken by such a high level politician, who also is from the "hard-headed" business world and is respected by it:

"There's no doubt," (Martin) now says, "that one of the greatest questions of our age is how the world is going to govern itself. And I believe the answer to that question is going to be decided over the course of the next 20 or 30 years . . ." In the face of globalization, national sovereignty will be preserved only if nation states get together and set the rules of the game because, he says, "if they don't put together the rules of the game, then large multinational institutions are going to run rampant." He talks about providing a kind of bankruptcy protection for countries. Instead of allowing a crisis to happen, its capital would be frozen, debts locked in and the economy reorganized . . . Why not welfare for the world? "We within our borders recognize that we have to have a basic level of welfare for the poorest of the poor in our country. We've got to recognize sooner or later that the same thing has to apply internationally."

Media

At present, we do not generally pay much serious attention to the impact of the media on society. There seem to be several reasons for this. The first and most important one is that any attempt to control the media immediately (and often justifiably) alarms defenders of Free Speech, especially in the U.S.A., where it is part of the Constitution. Secondly, most people associate the media with frothy and harmless TV entertainment—something with which to pass time, something to gossip about. Thirdly, in our current "scientism" way of looking at life, what is broadcast is not really "real" since you cannot touch it or show direct cause and effect. Fourthly, we feel we are in control because we can switch channels or websites or turn off altogether. Fifthly, the media industry is immensely powerful, controlling not only what is broadcast but exercising much direct influence on the government. Probably the most vocal groups at present are parents and certain religious organizations.

The Buddha, as we have seen, pointed out that we are the result of what we think, and in elaboration of this, he explained the dynamics of conditioning. His Noble Eightfold Path included Right Speech and Right Action, which entailed not merely refraining from lying and stealing, etc., but actually being constructive, peaceful, and honorable in our words and actions. Since we are all conditioned as well as conditioning, we should be aware of our speech and actions since they always have an impact on ourselves as well as others.

What the Buddha taught is not only still valid but also more apparent and urgent than ever since realistic sounds and images can be received (often uninvited) in the privacy of our homes. Although the framers of the American First Amendment were brilliant in their own time, they possessed neither the deep psychological and spiritual insight of the Buddha nor the foresight to anticipate our current technological capabilities. The effect of individuals speaking their minds in the town square, town hall, bar, or rudimentary newspaper is quite different from a continuous barrage of sounds and images from the TV or computer screen received in the seeming privacy and security of your home from the very earliest age. Moreover, these messages are often reinforced through other media like magazines, music, videos, films etc. Many children now spend far more time with the screen than with their parents, and as this screen time becomes more interactive, it also becomes more "real"—in other words, "virtual reality." Since "virtual reality" will appear increasingly similar to "real" reality, this makes the question, "What is reality?" all the more relevant and urgent.

Although the proverbial person-in-the-street still maintains that she or he is in control of and not unduly influenced by TV, movies, and the Internet, there is growing evidence to the contrary. The amount of time that we, and especially our children, are spending in front of the screen has been steadily increasing to the point of addiction. TV viewing patterns are studied closely by marketers (often with the help of psychological expertise) and even individual Internet activity may be tracked. Indeed, the contents of many computers are scanned via the Internet without their owners' knowledge. In short, we are being consistently and successfully manipulated to buy a wide variety of "products"—not only goods and services, but lifestyles, aspirations, ideas and emotions, including hatred.

Media education in schools should be an important and compulsory part of the basic curriculum since we obviously now live in an Age of Information. We are spending more time with machines and less with people, so it is prudent to be aware of the possible effects this has on us. As we have seen, the link between violence and video games has been established. A study conducted over fifteen years and published in 2003 by social psychologist Rowell Huesmann and colleagues at the University of Michigan found that both boys and girls who watched a lot of violence on TV between the ages of six and nine are more likely to behave violently as adults and are therefore more likely to be convicted of criminal behavior because of it. An earlier study by Huesmann had found harmful effects only for boys. Huesmann speculated, "It's possible that the feminist movement of the late '60s and '70s has made females less inhibited about expressing aggression. Also, there has been an increase in aggressive female role models on TV and in the movies."

When we begin to recognize the pervasive power of the media, we will choose more wisely what we (and our children) watch, and this in turn will have a dramatic effect on the type of programming offered to us by the media-entertainment industry. When violence, degradation, sexual preoccupation, unnatural body shaping, etc. are no longer regarded as "cool" and "sophisticated," the social pressure against them will build as it did with smoking and driving while under the influence of intoxicants. The quality of "mind food" that we ingest will be regarded as important as the quality of "body food."

As we are able to discern more subtle and complex patterns of cause and effect, this will be reflected in legal decisions and legislation. Lawsuits have already been filed against movie and video game makers by the parents of children who have died in high school slayings, inspired by specific movies and video games. Commenting on one of the lawsuits associate director of the American Civil Liberties Union Barry Steinhardt predictably stated, "There is no substantial social-science evidence that shows that entertainment causes violence. The people who commit violence should be held accountable, not the entertainment industry." The NRA made a similar argument against gun control. Such debates are still being cast in crude "either-or" terms rather than "both-and" which as we have seen would allow for more sophisticated examinations of specific situations.

Another area of the media, which has slipped by our monitoring antennae is advertising. It not only pays for a lot of media content but also has itself become part of the content, constituting a huge industry in its own right. On TV, the standard short ads have been joined by the longer "infomercials"; fashion magazine ads constitute the greater part of many fashion magazines; TV shows are made on the shooting of magazine photos or fashion shows. Like most of the media, advertising has been ignored as harmless fluff, but it plays an important role in shaping our lifestyle choices—skeletal or over-muscled body shaping, smoking, alcohol, drugs, sexual customs, SUVs, cosmetic surgery, cell phones, and consumerism in general—the recurrent American Dream. Advertising thus consumes enormous amounts of resources even as it persuades us to buy and use goods that we do not really need and that may even be harmful to us and to our environment. As such, it plays an extremely important and largely unregulated role in molding our lives.

I think the raising of advertising standards is necessary. One drastic but commonsense change would be to make advertising purely informative and ban all "lifestyle" advertising. A lesser change would be to feature actual users rather than actors in endorsement advertising such as, "I used this product and look what it did for me." For example, it seems not only absurd but fraudulent, for advertisements for weight loss supplements, foods, drinks, and exercise equipment to show beautiful young actors whose physiques have been enhanced through extensive weight training, steroids, and cosmetic surgery, especially breast implants. You are not going to get like that from taking a supplement. Advertisers who use surgically enlarged breasts to sell their particular product are also incidentally selling cosmetic surgery and unnatural body images. Another common example is "antiageing" products where often the models and actors used are years younger than the target audience. If someone is endorsing a product, it would seem reasonable to apply the simple cause-and-effect "reality" standard we apply to everything else. Why should something as influential as advertising get a "free pass"?

Other areas of the media that need scrutiny are news and politics, although these are more difficult to monitor and control. The false illusion of choice, impartiality, and balance in TV news programs is dangerous in a democracy, which is based on opinion. In the first place, producers and researchers define the topics and range of opinions beforehand, select the so-called experts in an arbitrarily and haphazard manner (in which I have much personal experience), while the interviewers or mediators keep the discussion within the agreed parameters. It all seems very objective, fair, and educational, but in fact the broad outlines of the outcome are predetermined. One of the main ground rules is to avoid upsetting viewers, who represent income, so the slant is often to support and reinforce status quo attitudes. This is commonly done by the interviewer interjecting personal "man in the street" anecdotes and comments. "Experts" are usually selected in terms of "for" or "against" (either-or). I have rarely, if ever, seen people on TV advocating "both-and" points of view. Perhaps the general public is considered incapable of understanding the latter, or perhaps producers prefer simplicity and the friction and tension of conflict— makes for better television ratings, as the so-called reality shows have proven!

The influence of television on national elections and politics in general has been growing appreciably, especially in the U.S.A. A decisive part of each presidential campaign takes place on TV— national ads, sound bites, "photo opportunities," debates, appearances on talk shows, etc. In these circumstances, media performance, physical appearance, and personality far outweigh intelligence, honesty, experience, and specific policies. The media can also arbitrarily make or break a story and thereby influence the political climate. The media's obsession with President Clinton's dalliance with intern Monica Lewinsky led to an impeachment that consumed much money and preoccupied the administration and both political parties for months. This led to the neglect of much more important matters, including the bombing of the U.S.S Cole, which was part of the al-Qaeda terrorist run up to September 11. This obsession was baffling since presidential lying and extramarital affairs have been common in the past. It takes on more sinister overtones when one considers that other presidents have lied with impunity about much more serious matters, including illegal and damaging covert operations and diversion of funds. In stark contrast to the scrutiny that Clinton got, the subsequent administration of George W. Bush seems completely immune to criticism despite repeated inaccuracies and self-contradictions, links to corporate criminals, past dealings with Saddam Hussein and much more.

In the eyes of the world (outside America), the U.S. media coverage of the last Iraqi War seemed like one long infomercial for the American military. Media outlets even repeated all the slogans and banner headlines fed to them by the military. For example, the war was called "Operation Iraqi Freedom" even though the initial reason for war was rooting out Islamic terrorists. When an Iraqi connection to al-Qaeda terrorists could not be proved, the rationale for war was suddenly changed to getting rid of "Weapons of Mass Destruction (WMDs)." Although UN weapons inspectors on the ground in Iraq could find no WMDs, Bush still sent troops in, suddenly switching his reasons for war to freedom and democracy. In fact, the decision to go to war was made virtually certain once troops were dispatched many months before combat began. Illegal bombing of Iraqi military installations was taking place even as America asked for UN blessing to go to war.

The Iraqi war has been by far the most "staged" in the Hollywood sense. "Embedded" journalists had to travel with American troops, agreeing to restrictions on what they could report; no pictures of American wounded or dead were allowed; body bags were renamed "transfer tubes." The propaganda machine created its ultimate Hollywood moment early in the military campaign, when the fighting was not going too well. Videotape on all the TV networks showed American troops in a daring nighttime raid, heroically rescuing Pte. Jessica Lynch, a pretty young blonde, whose photo was shown endlessly. The story circulated that she was among a group of American soldiers ambushed and captured. She was injured but fought until her ammunition ran out. She was raped and then imprisoned in an Iraqi hospital, from which she was heroically rescued nine days later. Her story was made into a movie.

In truth, her gun jammed and she never fired a shot. She lost consciousness for three hours when her vehicle crashed and knows nothing about a sexual assault. The hospital staff, who attended her were actually very kind and even offered her rescuers a key to where she was being kept. There were no soldiers at the hospital guarding her when the daring rescue was made. Canada's Toronto Star and then the BBC ran a more accurate account of the story shortly after it happened, but the American media did not take it up. Lynch was awarded a Bronze Star for bravery and a Purple Heart for being injured and was given 80 percent disability benefit. Shoshanna Johnson, a black woman who was injured and captured in the same convoy as Lynch's, got no medal and only 30 percent disability benefit. To her credit, the twenty-year old Lynch, once recovered, stood up and flatly contradicted the Pentagon's version of her story.

Mark Crispin Miller of New York University commented on the story:

> This White House believes that they can spin their way out
> of anything and they assume reality will surrender to their
> spin.

Veterans' groups complained about the Pentagon's glorification of Jessica Lynch and by association, the Iraqi war, while they prevented coverage of the growing numbers of dead and wounded. In addition, they were unhappy that wounded soldiers were not getting proper medical attention and support when they returned home.

The actual story of Jessica Lynch may not be important in itself but its coverage is part of what should be a disturbing trend of media "truth" manipulation. What is even more alarming is that the American public does seem to think this particularly important. It may be argued that the ongoing and widespread bending of "truth" by an American administration poses a greater long-term threat to American democracy than Saddam Hussein ever did. Marshall McLuhan pointed out decades ago that the "medium is the message," but the full implications of his insights are still largely unacknowledged. Hopefully, this will change with a shift in consciousness.

Health and Education

Health and education are obvious and promising areas of our lives for the application of the Ageless Wisdom because we can do it by ourselves, right here and now. Increased mind-body self-knowledge will radically and rapidly improve our health, vitality, and our relationships with others. Individuals who are healthy and balanced in mind and body not only represent enormous savings in social and financial remedial costs to society, but also provide it with the vision and purpose it so badly needs. Much of this knowledge can be taught at home and in our schools at little financial cost.

The most important lesson that we can learn and teach our children is that it is possible to know oneself (and consequently know others) in a way that is significantly more profound, complex, and inclusive than current conventional wisdom. This knowledge will make us more self-sufficient and at the same time more open to community and to sharing. In a sense, if we each take off our distorting goggles, we will see the same thing. We will start paying attention to the *quality* of what we absorb into our bodies, hearts, and minds and also to our own words and actions, since we will see for ourselves, their subtle and far-reaching effects.

Knowledge in the above context may often mean going against the conventional tide, but it does not mean saying or doing whatever you feel like, which is mere narcissism and selfishness. Neither is it the same as belief-driven religion and ideology, as has been explained.

Since there are no scientific or other comprehensive studies (to my knowledge) on raising children according to Ageless Wisdom principles, I will offer hereunder a short summary of my experiences and impressions with my own daughters, who are presently aged 22, 20, and 17.

When I was about to become a parent, I read several helpful birthing and child care books, but I could not find anything, which explained modern parenting in Buddhist or Daoist terms. There was a lot of psychology but no coherent spirituality. Religious books for children merely told simplified biblical stories with pictures. I figured that I could not go far wrong if I started off with love and the reassurance of my physical presence and touch, which was what I gave them.

I could spend my days with my children since I worked mostly at night. I regarded this as a valuable, albeit non-monetary, benefit of my career move from the business world to teaching. It did not pay the bills but allowed me to be with my children in their formative years. I fed them, changed diapers, and even weaned them from their mother's breasts, since she could not stand their heartbreaking, nightlong crying. When they began their schooling, I would often take them to parks, the beach, petting zoos, etc., after school. No monetary value can be attached to such moments even though they have remained vivid in all our memories. Sadly, many in our present society regard such activities as time wasting and therefore worthless. There is no societal reward for being a good person, much less a good parent. Indeed, if you are in the conventional work force and want to take time off for your family, you are often prevented or penalized formally or informally. The present competitive system encourages others to take advantage of your perceived "laziness," "lack of drive," "not being a team player," etc.

All my children, in their early years, were affected far more by emotions than by reasons and explanations and all could feel, without any prompting, the movement of subtle energy (qi or prana). My first memorable experience with emotions occurred when my first daughter, Shu-wen, was only a few months old. One day, after hours of her intermittent crying and fretting, I became frustrated and yelled at her to stop crying. She screamed in pain as if I had physically hit her, even though I was across the other side of the room! After this, I was much more careful with my emotional state around her (and subsequently her sisters), and in this undertaking, my meditation practice came in very useful. Children often read your true emotional state even if you pretend to be happy, which thus sends confusing, mixed messages to them. It also teaches them to suppress and cover over emotions.

Because I was deliberately low-key (yet supportive) in stressful situations, I made an interesting discovery regarding my children's reaction to physical pain. I noticed that from an early age, when they hurt themselves by falling or bumping into things, they would instantly look at me before reacting, as if asking for my guidance. Instead of jumping up in alarm, I would calmly go to them, ask if they were okay, and reassure them. More often than not, there would be no tears. When my youngest, Hana, was only about a year old, she fell down a full flight of stairs, tumbling like a ball and then slamming onto the floor. Looking over at her, I saw her staring at me in surprise. I strolled over to her, comforted her, and took her back upstairs where she continued playing, without shedding a tear. When Shu-wen was about 6 years old, she had about 5 stitches in her lip without anesthetic and without crying. Whenever my children were around adults who showed alarm and panic, they would tend to react more like "ordinary" children and would cry and fuss more if they had even a minor accident. I remember one of Hana's friends, at about the age of 7, stumbling and bumping her knee on our carpeted floor then screaming as if she had broken her leg. I asked her why she was crying since she did not seem to suffer any real hurt. She explained that when you hurt yourself, you are "supposed to cry."

Even when they were seriously hurt and in pain, like the time my second daughter Shu-wei was deeply gashed in the forehead by a falling ice shovel or Hana fractured her leg, I remained calm, hugged and comforted them, and advised them to relax and *accept* the pain (the Buddha's non-attachment) since what happened could not be undone. I sympathized with their pain but pointed out that pain, like pleasure, was something natural that comes and goes. I asked them to observe and verify for themselves whether they feel better fighting and crying or relaxing and accepting the fact of their injury. After experimenting for themselves, they all agreed that acceptance was better. I deliberately refrained from distracting them or bribing them with candy or toys when they were hurt (or bored), because I felt that reinforced the dualistic view of life as good and bad—running in circles towards the good and away from the bad. I think the practice of dentists giving

candy and sweets to kids as a reward after treatment is a supreme
example of the contradictory, circuitous mixed message—"Candy
rots your teeth, and I have just painfully repaired the damage so I
will reward you with some candy."

Handling emotional pain is not very different from handling
physical pain. I advised them to first accept what had happened
and to feel the pain, keeping their hearts open so that their emotions
could flow through without building up, especially negative
emotions like anger, fear or sadness. The next step was to find
"right action"—how to respond in the present moment to what
had happened. I advised them to ask themselves the question, "What
do I need to do now?" rather than "What do I want?" I cautioned
that accepting the reality of what has happened is not the same as
accepting the "rightness" of that action. For example, if someone
hurts you and it is a single occurrence, you can let go of the pain
and move on. If you are in a continuing relationship, however, and
that hurt is being repeated, then the situation must be resolved. If
it is that person's behavioral or personality pattern to hurt, you are
not doing that person a service by letting her or him keep on
hurting you.

All of this seemed to make sense to them and they could from
a very young age check the condition of their hearts by "looking
into it," sometimes accompanied by graphic images. They could
observe and conclude for themselves whether their hearts were open
or closed. When their hearts were closed, they would experience
more emotional complications and physical discomfort, mostly in
the chest area but sometimes in other parts of the body as well.
When they opened their hearts, letting go of negative emotions,
their pain and resentment would vanish almost immediately. I
thought this was the best form of teaching because it was from
their direct experience. It taught me too because I usually work on
such matters with adults rather than children.

One day in March 1993, when they were 11, 9, and 6,
following a screaming argument between all three, I offered to
trade them an hour-long "timeout" in their rooms for a briefer
period of formal standing meditation. To my surprise, they agreed,

and although they had never tried it before, all stood very still with their eyes closed for between 10-20 minutes, which in my experience, most adults find very difficult. To my continuing astonishment, they subsequently reported that they actually enjoyed the experience because it made them feel relaxed, calm, and loving. Their previous bickering had evaporated, and they voluntarily apologized to me and to each other. I seized on all the love and goodwill flowing from them and offered to sit in meditation with them each day. They thought that was a great idea, and we all followed through on it.

About a month later, out of the blue, their mother announced that she wanted to separate from me permanently after eighteen years of marriage and twenty-three years of being together. We were all extremely shocked since there had been no quarrels between us. The next few months were difficult and painful. In hindsight, however, the breakup went comparatively smoothly, and I credit that to the groundwork that we had previously done on "letting go" and acceptance as well as our recent formal periods of meditation together. Our daily sessions allowed us to acknowledge our pain, keep our hearts open, talk with, and comfort each other. I am eternally thankful for the "coincidence" that started us meditating. Even after I left the home, they continued to meditate daily together for a few months and then individually, as they grew older and developed different habits and groups of friends.

All of my children from an early age could feel subtle energy (Qi). When I ran healing energy through their bodies (sometimes without touching), they were able to describe the precise pathways of the energy that I was silently visualizing. I usually did this for minor ailments like bumps, cuts, headaches, and stomachaches. Having repeatedly experienced fast relief and recovery, they not only trusted it but also asked for it when hurt. Sometimes the injuries were more serious. While I was on San Juan Island studying with my meditation teacher, Dhiravamsa, Shu-wen, who was two years old, fell and gashed her forehead at least a centimeter deep. Since it was difficult to get medical attention there, I healed her energetically. The cut quickly stopped bleeding and closed up, leaving no scar. Later in Toronto when she was about 10, she got poked in her eye with a sharp stick while playing with a friend in the garden. The eye specialist predicted at least a 60 percent loss of vision in the eye. I worked energetically on her eye several times a day before her next appointment a few days later. When the doctor saw her, he was shocked the eye had unexpectedly and miraculously healed.

My second daughter, Shu-wei, was particularly sensitive to energy even if it was directed at her (without warning or outward sign from me) from across the room. Around the age of ten, after one of her ballet classes, she casually related to me that, in order to help one of her friends appear to be working hard at ballet (and therefore appease their strict teacher), she made her so hot with Qi that her friend turned red and started to sweat. Her friend was amazed (as was I) and asked what happened. Shu-wei told her it was just a trick. She later explained to me that since her friends did not believe in things like Qi and energy, she did not bother to tell them.

I did not formally discuss morality or spirituality with my daughters unless they asked me or a particular situation called for it—friendship, lying, sharing, conflict, religious holidays, etc. I openly discussed pain, sickness, loss, old age, and death because I did not want to make those subjects taboo. I shared with them what I knew, and if I was talking about Buddhism and Daoism I would usually explain the equivalent perspective of Christianity, which had been the religion of my own childhood and was the dominant religion of Canada, the country of their birth and residence. If they expressed a particular belief or attitude, which I did not think was well founded, I would question them as to how they came up with that conclusion and would explore the implications of it both in terms of their own internal dynamics (i.e., how it would make them feel, think, and act) and their relationship with others.

When Shu-wei was about eight, she came home from school one day and immediately asked me what religion we were. She said almost all the kids in school believed in something, mostly

Jesus and Christianity. She asked whether we were Christians, Buddhists or what. I said I did not think it was necessary to believe in anything since if you blindly believed something, you did not really, directly know. If you knew, belief would not be necessary.

She did not fully understand this but suggested it was okay for one person to have one belief and another person to have a different belief. I agreed but cautioned that not all religions were necessarily equal in their effect. I pointed out by way of example that most Buddhists and Hindus probably regarded Jesus as an enlightened world teacher, like the Buddha and the Hindu saints. Many Christians, however, regard other religions as false or even evil and insist that Jesus is unique, being the one and *only* son of God. I pointed out that rigid religious beliefs have lead to wars and killings throughout history. This genuinely surprised and horrified her. The possibility had never crossed her mind that religion could lead to war.

She then asked what the Buddha taught about God. I said he advised that each person be her or his own refuge and that we should look inside for truth and to discover our true nature. The Buddha was a man, but a completely enlightened one. She agreed from her own experience that she could find out what was right by really looking inside. She added, however, that not all the voices she hears are true. She said that the false voices usually speak first and are located in the throat area, but if she takes the time to inquire further, she can find the true voice, which usually comes from the heart/chest area.

As my daughters entered their teenage years, they became more consumed by the time demands of schoolwork and socializing. Each of them was powerfully affected by peer pressure, not only through their own groups of friends but by the popular media culture. As we have seen earlier in this book, these phenomena are both powerful and widespread. Peer pressure is part of a development stage of consciousness (the need to function within a group), and this fact is being deliberately exploited by marketers, often aided by professional psychologists. My daughters' formal practice of meditation and Qigong dwindled, probably because it took discipline, time and was solitary, not a "cool," social activity. An additional factor in the case of my children was that after the marriage breakup, they continued to live with their mother (although we shared joint custody), whose lifestyle is much more conventional and affluent than mine. Their parental influences thus became markedly divided.

As I take stock of my experiences with my children thus far, there is nothing I would change. I am thankful for and enriched by three healthy, beautiful, loving, and affectionate daughters. They are all very vibrant and spirited. There is occasional friction resulting from personality differences and the daily stresses of life but no entrenched conflict or animosity. I have never felt any estrangement or distance from them. Their health and their school marks are above average, although university has been a struggle for Shu-wen. When she was about ten years old, I felt that something was not quite normal with her mental processing but her teachers assured me all was well because her marks were average or above. By chance, one of my Taijiquan students did educational testing and volunteered to test Shu-wen. As a result, it was discovered that she had a non-verbal learning disability, which doctors have linked to major hearing loss in her left ear, probably due to early childhood measles. This has caused her coordination difficulties, both physically and mentally, especially in sorting out complex activities and logical sequences. Her schooling has been normal except she needs tutorial help from time to time.

I feel that I have given my daughters valuable mind-body tools that they know are valid and effective. It is up to them if, how, and when they use them. When they are sick or having emotional problems, they often instinctively turn to meditation and Qigong, either doing Qigong exercises I have taught them or asking me for a Qigong treatment. Both Shu-wen and Shu-wei have in the past selected Buddhism as university and school projects and accept its fundamental tenets. They all get on well with friends of different religions and have attended their friends' respective places of worship.

When pressed, they do not make the excuse that they do not

know why they do or say certain things. They accept that body, energy, and mind are interlinked; they understand the consequences of emotional repression; they see that all humans are connected and are interdependent with the "external" world. All this is the result of their own experiences over time not because I have drilled my beliefs into them so they can parrot them back to me. It is far more than I was aware of at their age. One of the most valuable results of all this is that there are no entrenched conflicts between us. We have so far been able to substantially resolve our problems, to acknowledge what (internal) work still needs to be done and generally to be caring and loving to each other.

Based on my experience with my children as well as with thousands of adult students and patients, I am convinced that similar mind-body skills can be taught at schools for very little monetary cost. First, however, we need the collective will to do so. As we have repeatedly discussed throughout this book, postmodernism has frozen us into inaction in many areas of our lives, including (and especially) education. We are still largely stuck in political correctness—we are afraid to say anything about religion lest we offend; parents and teachers, not wanting to be "authoritarian," are afraid to act as parents and teachers, so try to be buddies and friends. If you are merely your child's friend, why should they listen to you any more than their other friends? Again, we can solve this problem if we think "both-and" instead of "either-or."

Teaching the Ageless Wisdom (as well as more specific courses, e.g., on personality types, health, and media manipulation) is not a threat to peace since it is not about building power or setting one faction against another. Its emphasis is on individual transformation, which in turn gives rise to compassion, wisdom, and a feeling of oneness. We undoubtedly cannot come to oneness by holding as "sacred" every aspect of our separateness. One of the simplest and most profound spiritual exercises we can start practicing is simply paying attention to what is taking place within ourselves, without any goals or preconceptions. I find it hard to imagine how this can be perceived as offensive, destructive, or evil but no doubt there are people who will find reasons. Hopefully as consciousness shifts, the number of such people will lessen. A more supportive and compassionate culture will in turn allow our children to blossom even more.

It is important that Ageless Wisdom disciplines be taught by those who know it through substantial study and experience. There is a strong bias in the West that all teaching, especially in formal institutions, must be done by those with "credibility" like academics, psychologists, doctors, etc. Thus, for example, western medical doctors can take weekend courses in acupuncture, Insight Meditation, etc., and then immediately use those disciplines within their profession, enabling their patients to claim it in their medical insurance plans. At the same time, the people who have devoted their whole lives to those disciplines (and may be the teachers of those medical doctors) are often denied the same opportunities because they have no "credibility" or "qualifications."

A shift in parenting and education as outlined above would dramatically and positively impact personal health. More self-knowledge (i.e., awareness of personal cause and effect) would lead to greater care in lifestyle habits and spending in matters such as food, recreation, exercise, sexual activity, relationships, and social drugs, including alcohol and tobacco. Instead of abusing ourselves and then expecting medicine to come up with a quick fix, magic bullet cure, we will begin to take responsibility for ourselves. Preventative health care can be a source of enormous savings and potential for society but at present is almost totally neglected since there is no profit in it for individuals and corporations. Governments may run token anti-smoking ads, but these are swamped by cigarette advertising and subtler but far more effective glamorizing of the practice in films, etc. Preventative health care is regarded as not "real" because we cannot see it (lack of sickness) and so does not merit funding. If, however, we abuse ourselves with drugs, alcohol, cigarettes, and food, falling physically ill, then that is "real" and thus deserves extremely expensive medical care!

Apart from stress, which we have already discussed, one of the most important factors affecting our health is food. This should not really be surprising since we are biochemical machines, and we put substantial amounts of food into our bodies at least three times a day, plus various "snacks" and drinks. We have become addicted to salt, sugar, fats, and animal products, all of which are relatively modern additions to the human diet and have been shown to be detrimental to our health in the inflated proportions we now consume. Both salt and sugar are usually present in most prepared foods, whether bought in the stores or in restaurants, and thus accumulate rapidly in our bodies. If we reduce these ingredients, it will not only improve our health, but we will find our taste buds becoming more alive and sensitive. There is much sweetness, for example, in organic fruit and even carrots. The more sensitive we become, the more we will appreciate quality in our food. The medical establishment is strangely quiet on the subject of eating habits, preferring to prescribe drugs—probably quicker for doctors, more money for the pharmaceutical companies, and less chance of being sued by food providers. In one high-profile case, TV celebrity Oprah Winfrey was (unsuccessfully) sued by Texas beef producers because she dared to link mad cow disease with beef.

Food intake is important not only in terms of the items we select but also in quality. For reasons of cost savings, appearance, and texture, most of the foods available to us contain pesticides, preservatives, and additives including hormones and antibiotics. Many of these man-made substances, together with the remnants of detergents, disinfectants, fire retardants, shampoos etc., remain in our water supply and food chain and accumulate in our bodies. Studies have linked many of these substances with serious diseases including cancer and infertility. With these issues still in the stage of denial, we are already plunging ahead with genetically modified foods, the implications of which are unknown. If all these items eventually prove to be detrimental to our health, I see no reason why the manufacturers of these contaminants, the food producers, the government, and the medical establishment should not all be

held legally responsible because persuasive evidence already exists
that many of these substances may be toxic. If you live and profit
by the lawsuit, you may die by the lawsuit (except corporations, of
course, which just dissolve and reform elsewhere).

In terms of systems reform, I think the general public would
benefit from impartial scrutiny of the self-regulating monopoly
granted to the medical establishment and its relationship with the
pharmaceutical (and more recently, bioengineering) industries. In
the Free Market environment, it is increasingly common for doctors
to accept benefits from drug companies and for the latter to fund
hospital and university projects. This is not conducive to
impartiality. Conventional medicine has been reduced to glorified
auto mechanics—run a scan, replace parts, change the fluids, adjust
the fuel mixture. Like the auto industry, the people making most
of the profits are the manufacturers who factor obsolescence and
dependent add-ons to their products. It is not uncommon for
pharmaceutical companies to market drugs that need other drugs
to combat their side effects or to create new markets for old drugs,
as in the sudden supposed epidemic of "generalized anxiety
disorder" (GAD). As in the legal system, money tilts the playing
field. This applies to the availability and quality of treatment as
well as the direction of medical research. For example, there is
much more profit in cosmetic surgery for the rich than in providing
relatively cheap and basic care for the poor masses.

In 2003, Canada took a pioneering step in limiting the
monopoly of the pharmaceutical companies. It amended its patent
laws to allow developing nations to import cheap drugs for the
treatment of AIDS, malaria, tuberculosis and other epidemics.

Another consequence of the monopoly granted to conventional
Western medicine is that other forms of healing and medicine have
been marginalized and, in some cases, demonized. The most
important advantage given to conventional medicine is that it is
covered by the major medical plans, including government. The
second advantage they have is legal and financial. When medical
associations go after practitioners of alternative medicine (including

conventional doctors) in the law courts, they benefit from a "credibility" bias and very deep pockets.

The third advantage is a popular media that is inclined to mock unconventional medicine. In this respect, a series of newspaper items a few months ago caught my attention. The first news item revealed that a study in the *Journal of the American Medical Association* concluded that between 5,000 to 15,000 hospital patients die each year because of medical errors. This followed an Institute of Medicine report in 1999 that estimated 98,000 hospitalized Americans die annually from medical mistakes. The second medical news item was local. A Toronto neurologist, whose clinics used dirty needles on patients, had caused the worst hepatitis B outbreak in Ontario, infecting 1,000 people and resulting in the death of one person. Both of the above items were covered by small columns in the inner pages of Toronto's major daily newspaper. I commented then to several of my students that such news items are normally underplayed whilst errors by practitioners of alternative medicine are magnified. A short time later, a local acupuncturist's reused needles caused a relatively minor skin infection in less than 20 patients. That story, sure enough, was reported in front page banner headlines in the same newspaper, spawned a $3 million lawsuit from one of the infected patients, and became "proof" of quackery in a number of websites devoted to disparaging complementary medicine.

A more enlightened and integral approach to medicine and health would include mind as well as body, Eastern as well as Western modalities, the subjective as well as the objective approach. As with other areas of our life, the subjective dimension has been almost totally neglected by modern medicine. Western doctors and researchers in various fields, however, are beginning to recognize the role and power of the mind in both illness and healing and are beginning to investigate complementary medicine after many decades of condemnation and disdain. This change has been largely sparked by substantial numbers of patients in the West seeking treatment from practitioners of complementary medicine, or in other words, voting with their wallets. An article in *The New England Journal of Medicine* reported that in the U.S.A.:

> Expenditures associated with the use of unconventional therapy in 1990 amounted to approximately $13.7 billion, three-quarters of which ($10.3 billion) was paid out of pocket. This figure is comparable to the $12.8 billion spent out of pocket annually for all hospitalizations in the United States.

Bill Moyers, writing from a decidedly Western perspective, discussed his acclaimed PBS TV series, *Healing and the Mind*:

> Two important questions shaped the series: How do thoughts and feelings influence health? How is healing related to the mind? We asked doctors in large public hospitals and small community clinics about healing and the mind in daily practice. We talked to people in stress reduction clinics and therapeutic support groups and learned about such techniques as meditation and self-regulation as well as regimens of diet and exercise . . . We traveled to China to experience a culture whose model of human health is so different from ours that my questions about the connection of mind and body could not be answered within its frame of reference . . . What is health? When curing seems impossible, as in the case of terminal cancer, can we yet hope for "wholeness," the root of "healing"? . . . We in the West do not have to give up our own proven resources in order to appropriate the best another culture has to offer; here may well be the crucible where East meets West to forge a new source of healing.

CONCLUSION

I have lived a full and fortunate life, for which I am extremely grateful. I am grateful for ample food, water, and for good health. I am grateful to have shelter from the cold and from the heat. I am grateful to have experienced the love of my parents, brothers, children, lovers, friends, teachers, and students. I am grateful that I am not hated (for the most part) because of my race and that I can express my opinions without being attacked or arrested. I am grateful for living on a lush and beautiful planet with such an astounding variety of flora, fauna, and human beings.

I am saddened that most people on this planet still struggle just to survive. I am saddened that the planet is being devastated and species are disappearing at such a rate, biologists are calling the phenomenon, "The Sixth Extinction." I am saddened that we still brutalize each other on such a massive scale. As time goes on, I find I have less choice in how I live. Yes, I can buy dozens of different types of cars, computers, cell phones, and running shoes, but it is difficult to find quiet, clean green spaces. It is impossible to find uncontaminated air, water, and food.

Most of our major collective problems are man made or more specifically, the result of human conflict and greed. The "winners" we so admire create vastly more losers, who invariably want to turn the tables. This constant struggle militates against cooperation and long-term goals. Each party fears that others will get a "competitive edge" and so the pace of competition increases, sometimes breaking out into open war. This dynamic applies at all levels—countries, corporations, groups, teams, and individuals; it applies in different spheres—military, economic, technological, religious, cultural, etc. It now even applies in intimate, personal relationships.

Many people consciously or subconsciously hope that technology will somehow solve all our problems. Technology, no matter how powerful, however, will not solve greed, fear, anxiety, dissatisfaction, frustration, hate, ignorance, grief, etc. Moreover, technology, as we have seen, consistently generates "unforeseen" problems and makes life more complex. We try to solve these new problems with even more technology and so the wheel spins ever faster. There is evidence that as we rely more on technology, we become lazier and less able, both in body and mind.

Our infatuation with and addiction to science and technology over the last few centuries has caused us to neglect our inner life, and as a result, a dangerous gap has opened up between our technological expertise and our subjective, spiritual expertise. It's not unusual to witness world leaders, controlling vast war machines that could devastate the whole planet, react like hurt, petulant children or like tribal leaders from three thousand years ago. The same could be said of CEOs of large corporations who control workforces of thousands or direct civilization-altering, scientific, and technological research.

The scientific approach trains us to examine and specialize in compartments of life, and as a consequence we tend to lack overall vision—an understanding of how all the other parts might be affected by our actions. Thus our actions tend to be shortsighted, both in terms of scope and time frame. One hand does not know (or maybe does not want to know) what the other is doing. The recent Iraqi war is a classic example of this. The initial military campaign, executed with an extremely high-cost, high-tech army, was a brilliant success. It is doubtful, however, if any of the causes given for going to war were justified and in some areas, the threats have increased. No "weapons of mass destruction" were found even though we were assured we were in imminent danger of attack; terrorism is on the rise in Iraq with militants pouring in from other countries; the hope of a free, democratic Iraq remains distant; American soldiers are dying daily and the cost of the war keeps mounting. President Bush basks in the glory of being a "war leader" but other people die and pay the bills. Maurice Strong, special envoy to the U.N. secretary general Kofi Annan, noted, "Outsiders who have a fight with the U.S. will find co-operation among some Iraqis because there is significant resistance to the American occupation . . . Iraq was not a terrorist threat before the war but the U.S. has now made it a center of terrorism. There's the paradox."

The cost of the war and its aftermath is estimated at several hundred billion dollars. With that money (or less), America could have fulfilled its obligations under the Kyoto Protocol, and the world's atmosphere would be a lot cleaner. As a direct result of the war, the world's atmosphere is far filthier and of course, no country takes responsibility for cleaning it up. The average American taxpayer will foot the bill for the war (as well as additional interest on the national debt) while the big oil and weapons companies will get the lucrative contracts for rebuilding and rearming. Part of these profits will go back into more lobbying— in other words, using the people's money to get even more money from them.

It is commonly argued that since the Human Drama has played itself out for thousands of years, our present era is no different and that things will sort themselves out. What is unique about our era, however, is the scale and speed with which we are manipulating the environment and ourselves, which is a direct result of the development of modern science. We think of the earth as vast, but it is finite. The human population, with fast-growing needs and expectations, is exploding and has reached a level that far exceeds past historical levels. Many diverse forces are pushing us to ever faster and more radical scientific and technological innovation, the implications of which are moving beyond the comprehension of many specialists, much less the average person, which would include the average politician or lawyer or judge. There is much speed and activity but little sense of long-term direction, purpose or the Sacred.

The technologies of the twenty-first century will focus on the manipulation of our world at the microscopic level—bioengineering, genetics, and nanotechnology—and on robotics. We are already experimenting with man-made viruses, genetic modification, cloning, robotic implants, etc., which will vastly expand the potential for error and terror without necessarily increasing the quality of life. AIDS, SARS, West Nile disease, mad cow disease, and the 2003 Black Out of the North American east coast, affecting 50 million people, are not just bad luck but a harbinger of things to come. All of the above demonstrate the fact that we are unavoidably interconnected—not only human beings but all species—and that the speed and scope of any mishap or outbreak is rapidly increasing. There is no place to hide from our collective follies.

If we want to change the direction in which our collective lives are developing, we must radically change our attitudes and approach, or in other words, we must change ourselves at a profound level. We cannot change by holding on to all our old beliefs and institutions; we cannot change by insisting that we should always hold the upper hand or that others change first; we cannot change without self-knowledge because the self is our collective blind spot. Change in this context means the transformation or shifting of consciousness, which is far more profound than learning how to use a cell phone, DVD, or computer, drinking wine instead of beer, or getting accustomed to new sexual practices or gender roles.

Ageless Wisdom teachers have for millennia taught why and how we should transform our consciousness, but their message was little understood. At present there are certainly the needs and perhaps the circumstances for such a transformation to take place on a wider scale. It is unlikely that in the next few decades we will be transformed into a planet of Buddhas. Even if we just begin to realize, however, that we are indeed connected with all beings, and we begin to see how those connections operate, the power of that realization will far exceed even the most fantastic technological invention. If the quality of human decision making and caring goes up by even a small percentage, it will be multiplied by a factor of many billions, representing not only the number of people in the world but the positive, reciprocating effect we will have on each other. In other words, it would be the reversal of the proverbial "vicious cycle."

Among the main reasons that human beings now rule the earth are their adaptability and their intelligence. We have spent the last few centuries making our machines more adaptable and intelligent, but have neglected ourselves. We are already heavily dependent on our machines not only for convenience but even survival. If we could respond more aptly, spontaneously, and harmoniously to life, we would not need so many machines, drugs, implants, therapists, "experts," "leaders," laws, weapons, etc. Life would become simpler and more peaceful; we would not need to fill our inner emptiness with activity and stimulus. With greater insight, we would find better avenues and applications for our scientific and technological genius.

At present, we rely on belief rather than direct, subjective understanding. Belief comes from the outside—religion, political party, "business," government, the media, etc.—and is by its nature rigid. It does not adapt quickly (or at all) and thus it can be both cumbersome and divisive. For example, most religious people are good, well-meaning people, but if they hold to a rigid belief in their own exclusive righteousness, that belief will lead them to war . . . just as in the past. The same holds true of any form of belief, not just religious.

A transformation of consciousness will give greater prominence to the subjective but will not lead to greater chaos and conflict because connection and integration are intrinsic parts of the new consciousness. We will understand how all the different parts within ourselves—body, emotions, mind, spirit—are connected and how we in turn are connected with our external environment. This being the case, we will realize that we cannot really "get away" with anything or get something for nothing; we will cease drawing arbitrary lines between the saved and the damned, the righteous and the unrighteous.

In order to transform our consciousness, we must start to look inside with skill, perseverance, and courage. We have to learn to value quiet, aloneness, and the profundity of doing absolutely nothing. In time, fear and hatred will fall away and be replaced by love and wisdom. Nothing is more valuable. It is the true promise of human evolution. The learned and insightful Huston Smith writes about the Ageless (Primordial) Wisdom in his book, *The Forgotten Truth*:

> What sets us against modernity is its demeaning of the human potential. The primordial tradition holds that man—not man in some hypothetically envisioned future, but man as he is constituted today and has always been constituted—is heir to *Sat, Chit* and *Ananda*: Infinite Being, Infinite Awareness, Infinite Bliss. It is impossible in principle for any alternative, ancient or modern, to match that claim, for if it did, in essence it would *be* the primordial philosophy, however different in details.

CHRONOLOGY OF
THE AGELESS WISDOM

Hereunder is a selected and abbreviated religious chronology with an emphasis on Ageless Wisdom Spirituality and Mysticism. Dates are approximate; historical milestones are included.

2000 BCE

- Shamanism is common worldwide.
- Pyramid building in Egypt has just ended. Stonehenge is under construction
- Legendary Period in China is credited with producing the *Yellow Emperor's Classic of Internal Medicine* and Yin-Yang theory.
- Early artifacts from the Indus Valley in India suggest that some form of yoga is already being practiced.

1500 BCE

- In India, early *Vedas* (Hindu scriptures) are being written down, having been previously passed down orally. They reflect the impact of the Ayran invasion from Persia (Iran), featuring sacrifices, prayers, chants and rituals directed at Aryan gods, including Indra, Mithra and Varuna. The Aryan caste system is adopted. The later *Vedas* feature spells, incantations, the healing use of herbs and astrology, which will form the basis of Ayurveda medicine.

1200 BCE

- Zoroaster in Persia introduces for the first time the notion of a one-time Creation, Fall and Redemption. Other details of his teachings would later be echoed in Judaism, including one transcendent god, angels and devils, Judgment Day, heaven and hell. Some sources place him as late as 600 BCE with the other Axial Sages (see below)

900 BCE

- The earliest Hebrew texts, which form the basis of the Biblical Books of Genesis and Exodus, are written down. The Yahwist Text (J), from the southern kingdom of Judah, is the earliest, followed nearly a century later by the Elohim Text (E), which originates in the northern kingdom of Israel.

700 BCE

- Founding of Rome and Greek City states, the most powerful being Athens and Sparta.
- The *Upanishads,* also known the *Vedanta* or the end of the *Vedas*, introduce a much more mystical and evolved concept of the Divine. They are widely considered to be the earliest and most comprehensive exposition of Ageless Wisdom spirituality. God is seen as not only transcendent but also immanent. The *Upanishads* explore the practice of yoga and the relationship of the individual self or *atman* with the greater Self.
- The yogic system is quite developed by the time the *Upanishads* emerge and is systematized by Kapila (around

600 BCE), founder of the Sankhya philosophy. The yoga system is further refined by Patanjali some time between 200 BCE and 300 CE.

600 BCE

- The "Axial Age" produces a comparative explosion (over two hundred years) of the world's greatest spiritual teachers and philosophers. They introduce novel ideas like the Wheel of Rebirth, enlightenment and the release of the soul back into the Eternal.
- In India, Mahavira (540-485 BCE) establishes Jainism, which is ascetic and sees spirit as imprisoned by matter. He preaches escape from the desires of the everyday world together with nonviolence to all beings, including insects.
- The Gautama Buddha (563-483 BCE) is now widely regarded as having cut through to the highest elements of Hinduism. His Middle Way is a new doctrine, which moves away from the dualism of the Sankhya system and from Vedic ritual, sacrifice and superstition.
- In China, Kong Fuzi or Confucius (551-497 BCE) emerges as China's "First Teacher," distilling the wisdom of its Legendary Period. Laozi, the supposed author of *Daodejing*, which in time becomes the main inspiration of Philosophical Daoism, is thought to have been a contemporary of Confucius. Confucius' teaching is predominantly ethical while Laozi's is more transformative. Confucianism, Daoism and later, Buddhism, will together shape China over the millennia.
- The Hebrew prophets, Isaiah and Jeremiah, preach a form of ethical monotheism.
- The first philosophers emerge in Greece. Pythagoras (582-500 BCE), part of the Dionysian Orphic movement, teaches a philosophy that resembles Vedanta.

500 BCE

- Pythagoras is followed by Heraclitus (544-480), Socrates (470-399) and Plato (427-347). Greek Mystery Schools arise. Greek thought and practice from this period will later have a profound influence on Western philosophy and mysticism.
- Rome becomes a republic.

400 BCE

- Alexander the Great expands the Greek Empire east to India, increasing the interchange between East and West.

300 BCE

- Zhuangzi. His teachings become a classic of Daoism, almost on par with *Daodejing*.
- In India, Ashoka enlarges his empire (268-232) and, disenchanted with war, converts from Hinduism to Buddhism. Buddhism flourishes in India and Buddhist teachers travel to Ceylon, Syria, Egypt and Greece

200 BCE

- Greece falls to Rome

0

- Jesus is widely regarded by Jews in Palestine as the Messiah prophesied by Isaiah. The earliest Christians consider themselves a Jewish sect. The New Testament Gospels of Matthew, Mark and Luke are subsequently written. around 70 CE.

100 CE

- Gnostic Christian sects are very popular. Gnosticism is mystic in flavor, reflecting Oriental and Greek "Mystery" influences. It includes the theology of (divine) immanence, which is regarded as heretical. The Roman Empire is at its apex.

- Mahayana Buddhism flowers as Buddhism spreads along the Silk Road to China. It emphasizes lay spirituality and devotion (the Heart). One of the most important Mahayana works is Nagarjuna's *Prajnaparamita Sutra*, which is translated into Chinese around 172 CE. This work will later influence *Chan* (Zen) and Tibetan Buddhism and is regarded as the source of eastern Nondual spirituality. *Nirvana* and *samsara* (the illusionary, everyday world) are not separate; one does not have to shun the world in order to be enlightened.
- Jerusalem is destroyed and the final Diaspora occurs, scattering the Jews around the Mediterranean.

200

- Plotinus integrates Plato's ideas with a variety of both Eastern and Western spiritual and philosophical teachings. He is regarded as the West's first teacher of Nondual spirituality and subsequently influences Western thinking down the ages. He attacks the Gnostics for shunning the everyday world as evil. Plotinus is very close in time to Nagarjuna, the first great Nondual teacher in the East.

300

- Christianity is allowed in the Roman Empire, which is on the decline.
- The controversial Nicene Creed is adopted by first Council of the Christian Church. Creation *ex nihilo* and the recognition of Jesus as the only Son of God become official Christian doctrine. Gnosticism is declared heretical.
- Saint Augustine, a follower of Plato and Plotinus, is converted to Christianity and becomes one of its greatest theologians.
- Height of Mayan empire in Mexico, Guatemala and Honduras.

400

- The Roman Empire splits into West and East, with the capitals being Rome and Constantinople (Istanbul) respectively. Christianity becomes the official religion of the Roman Empire. Atilla the Hun invades Gaul (France) and Italy in 452. The last Roman emperor is killed by Barbarians.
- Buddhism arrives in Japan

500

- *Bhagavad Gita* is composed and in time becomes the single most influential work in Hinduism.
- Bodhidharma comes from India to teach at the Buddhist Shaolin Temple in Henan Province, China. This gives rise to *Chan* (Zen) Buddhism and also to a martial arts system that spreads throughout the Far East.
- Split between Eastern and Western Christian churches. The former is often called the Orthodox Church and survives together with the eastern (Byzantine) Empire. The Eastern church begins to produce influential mystics like Saint Dionysius the Areopagite, also called Pseudo-Dionysius.
- *Sefer Yezirah* (The Book of Creation), one of the earliest texts of Jewish "Throne Mysticism" is written.

600

- Muhammad receives revelations from Allah, which form the basis of the Koran and his preaching. He sees himself as the final Semitic prophet in a line that includes Abraham, Moses, and Jesus. He is therefore called "The Seal of the Prophets". Originally, Muslims pray facing Jerusalem but Muhammad later changes the direction to Mecca. He sees Muslims as descendants of Abraham's son, Ishmael. Before establishing themselves in Mecca, Muhammad and his followers literally have to battle for survival.

- Shortly after Muhammad's death in 632, his successors (*kalipha* or caliphs) begin to spread Islam, initially among Arabs, through the strength of their armies. Early political squabbles lead to the Sunni and Shiah sects.
- Buddhism becomes the official religion in China and in Japan.
- Puranic period of Hinduism begins. It becomes more theistic, influenced by western religions and especially by Islam. Vishnu and Shiva are worshiped like monotheistic gods.
- Tantric practices begins to spread into both Hinduism and Buddhism.

700

- Islamic armies, with the help of conquered and converted recruits, spread the Islamic empire to Spain, North Africa, Persia, Jerusalem, India, and the borders of China. Civil war begins to divide the Islamic empire.
- Huineng (638-713), one of the greatest Chinese *Chan* Patriarchs.

800

- Sankara rekindles Hinduism with his Advaita (Nondual) philosophy, which is based on the *Upanishads* but shows the influence of the Buddhist Nagarjuna. Advaita is the realization that the ordinary individual is not separate from God, Brahman, the Eternal.
- Sufism is emerging. The Sufis see the Koran in more mystical, universal and inclusive terms than the majority of Muslims. Their emphasis is on the interior life and self-transformation, using techniques like night vigils, fasting and chanting. They develop the idea of approaching God as a lover. God is identified with the inner self and the source of being.

1000

- The Sufi al-Hallaj is crucified for in 992 for declaring, "I am the Truth."
- Marpa and Milarepa combine local shamanism, Tantra and Buddhism to create Tibetan Buddhism
- In Europe, religious intolerance leads to the persecution of Jews, not only because they are non-Christian but also because they are blamed for the death of Jesus. The Jews live mostly in Spain (Sephardim) and Germany (Ashkenasim). They flee east to Poland and Lithuania and to Spain, where the Islamic Moors are tolerant of them.

1100

- Christian knights begin the Crusades in an attempt to recapture the "Holy Land" of Palestine from the Muslims. The whole of Europe is now Christian.

1200

- The fourth Crusaders sack Constantinople because of doctrinal disputes.
- Eisai and Dogen bring Chan/Zen Buddhism to Japan. This coincides with the reign of the Shoguns, supported by the Samurai, which will last seven hundred years.
- The period of the great Sufi teachers, Ibn al-Arabi and Rumi, poet and founder of the *Mawlawiyyah* or Whirling Dervishes. His poem, the *Masnawi,* is later called the "Sufi Bible." In some countries, Sufism becomes the dominant sect.
- Jewish mysticism begins to grow among the Jews in the Islamic empire, partly in response to the rise of Islamic mysticism. Called the Kabbalah, it is influenced by the earlier Jewish Throne Mysticism and, like the Sufis, by Gnostic and Neoplatonic ideas. The *Zohar* is written in Spain and becomes the most important Kaballist work. The Moors in Spain begin to turn on the Jews.

- The Inquisition is established by Pope Gregory the Ninth. Over time it is used against Jews, mystics, witches and science.
- Thomas Aquinas (1225-74) attempts to integrate the philosophy of Augustine with that of the ancient Greeks, especially Aristotle. During this period, Arab translations of Greek philosophy are being retranslated into Latin and thus become available to Northern Europe.
- In 1199, Muslim raiding parties destroy the Buddhist university of Nalanda and kill 6000 monks. This helps to wipe out Indian Buddhism, which had been on the decline.

1300

- England becomes the first country to expel Jews. The Crusades end.
- Christian mysticism in Northern Europe grows, following a similar path to that trod by the Byzantine Christians, Sufis and Kabbalists before them. The most famous is the German, Meister Eckhart, who is influenced by Saint Dionysius.
- Aztecs are flourishing in Mexico and the Incas in Peru.
- First Christian missionaries arrive in China
- Islam becomes conservative as the study of the Holy Law (*Shariah*) is emphasized and new thinking is discouraged. Sufism declines. Islam is still the world's greatest power.

1400

- Ottoman Turks take Constantinople and destroy the Byzantium Empire. The Greek Orthodox tradition is carried on in Russia.
- The Renaissance starts as scholars begin to study the ancient Greeks and Romans, threatening the control on art and learning that the Roman Catholic Church imposes.

1500

- Martin Luther sparks the Protestant reformation, emphasizing faith rather than the sale of indulgences (forgiveness from the Roman Catholic Church).
- Inquisition is used as a weapon of the Counter Reformation, targeting the early scientists and mystics like St. Teresa of Avila.
- Isaac Luria develops a new mystical Kabbalah.
- Columbus and Cabot discover the Caribbean (1492) and North America (1497) respectively. Conquests by Spain in Central and South America follow. Christianity is spread. The African slave trade begins.
- Jesuit missionaries arrive in Japan.
- In Spain, the Muslims are expelled and the Jews are given the choice of conversion to Christianity or expulsion.
- Guru Nanak is the founder of Sikhism.

1600

- Wars of religion between Catholics and Protestants
- Galileo proves Copernicus' theory that the Earth revolves around the sun, contradicting the Church. He is tried and imprisoned for heresy but from that moment, the Church and religion generally are in retreat before the advances of modern science.
- Colonialism, enabled by powerful navies, spreads European culture, technology and Christianity worldwide. England claims North America and Australia.

1700

- The English mystical poet, William Blake, rebels against the sterility of the Age of Reason and against Christianity.
- Republics are established in America and France.
- The first steam engine is invented.

1800

- British "Orientalists" begin to translate Sanskrit and Pali texts, sparking Western interest in Buddhism and the more philosophical aspects of Hinduism, especially the *Upanishads* and the Advaita-Vedanta of Sankara. Madam Blavatsky and Colonel Olcott form the Theosophical Society, which spreads Indian forms of Ageless Wisdom in the West. In India, Hinduism is revitalized by teachers like Ramakrishna and his disciple, Vivekananda, who brilliantly introduces Hinduism to the world at the first World's Parliament of Religions, held in Chicago in 1893.
- American mystics include Black Elk, Walt Whitman and Ralph Waldo Emerson.
- Slavery is abolished and the first free settlers arrive in Australia.
- In 1856, Louis Pasteur discovers that bacteria cause disease.
- The world's population explodes and passes the billion mark for the first time.

1900

- Communism is established in Russia and becomes a major twentieth century force.
- The growing technological power and interdependence of nations produce the first World Wars and the use of Weapons of Mass Destruction, including Allied "carpet bombing", chemical warfare, German rockets and American atomic bombs, which wipe out Nagasaki and Hiroshima.
- During the Second World War, the Jewish Holocaust occurs and largely as a result of this, the Jews are given Israel as a permanent home. This in turn becomes a major source of conflict in the Middle East, feeding Islamic fundamentalism.
- Major political achievements (in some countries) include equal voting rights and opportunity for women and racial

minorities. After the Second World War, the United Nations becomes a global force and colonial independence accelerates.

- For the first time, environmental pollution and natural resources scarcity become a global problem. World population exceeds six billion.
- The growing and widespread intermixture of Eastern and Western thought produces many brilliant minds and spiritual teachers including Carl Jung, Albert Einstein. Ramana Maharshi, Krishnamurti, Aurobindo, Mahatma Gandhi, D.T. Suzuki, and many more.